LOST LEGACY

LOST LEGACY

❧

INSPIRING WOMEN *of* NINETEENTH-CENTURY AMERICA

Susan Flagg Poole, Editor

Foreword by Cecile Andrews

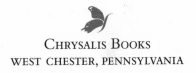

CHRYSALIS BOOKS
WEST CHESTER, PENNSYLVANIA

Library of Congress Cataloging-in-Publication Data
Lost legacy : inspiring women of nineteenth-century America / Susan Flagg Poole, editor.
 p. cm.
Includes bibliographical references
ISBN 0-87785-386-X
 1. Swedenborgian women—United States—19th century—biography.
I. Poole, Susan Flagg, 1948–   .
BX8747.L67   1999
289'.4'092273–dc21   99–35264
 [B]   CIP

Art Credits
Cover and frontispiece: Swedenborgian women in a private concert. Alice Sewall plays the viola. From collection of Susan Flagg Poole.
Photograph of Lydia Maria Child, page 2, courtesy of Art Resource, New York
Photograph of Sarah Orne Jewett, page 36, courtesy of Art Resource, New York
Photograph of Jesse Willcox Smith, page 46, and poster "Interchurch World Movement," page 53, courtesy of Delaware Art Museum, Wilmington, Delaware
Cover of *Little Women*, page 50, from the collection of the Brandywine River Museum (Chadds Ford, PA), Gift of the Women's Club of Ardmore, Haverford, Pennsylvania
Photographs of Lydia Fuller Dickenson, page 58, and Mary Lathbury, page 76, courtesy of General Convention, Swedenborgian Church, Newton, Massachusetts

Edited by Mary Lou Bertucci
Designed by Gopa Design, Fort Bragg, CA
Set in Bembo by Gopa Design

Printed in the United States of America

Chrysalis Books is an imprint of the Swedenborg Foundation.
For more information, contact:
Swedenborg Foundation Publishers
P.O. Box 549
West Chester, PA 19380
(800) 355-3222; Fax: (610) 430-7982
Web address: http://www.swedenborg.com

CONTENTS

FOREWORD

by Cecile Andrews

How did we become who we are? Did we choose our path in search of wealth and status? Did we choose our path to please our parents and teachers? Or did we simply fail to choose?

Few are happy and inspired in their careers. Too often we have charted our course with no sense of vision, with no sense of the exciting, transformative experience that a life work can be.

Why? Lots of reasons, of course—in a society devoted to the "bottom line," we are all affected. It is hard to remember that we are living for more sublime reasons than money and status. But as our society continues to break down, we see that our commercialized, consumerist, competitive society is exhausting us. We're often overcome with anxiety. We wake at three in the morning wondering what the boss meant by his or her comments at the staff meeting. Too many of us live in dread of emotional abuse—an employer who finds fault, a supervisor who retaliates. People are afraid they will lose their jobs if they speak up, so they compromise their integrity, pretending to go along.

People want a different path! We are all looking for passion and aliveness—work, whether paid or not, that brings a sense of meaning and joy. Some hope to start entirely new careers; others just want a way to renew themselves after a soul-draining day. But instead of moving ahead, we feel frustrated—we have not learned how to go about discovering our passion. Our schools rarely teach us, and our society rarely encourages us.

The modern women's movement encouraged many of us to break out of conventional molds, to try something other than teaching or nursing. Many of us wanted more than just individual change; we wanted to "reform the system" as well. But, unfortunately, the system reformed many of us. We tried to make a difference when we became lawyers and doctors, but too often we found ourselves working for giant corporations, rewarded only by wealth and status.

But now that these rewards have proven to be empty, where shall we turn to find our way?

Learning about people in history can change our lives. We need stories of real people to inspire us, to expand our sense of the possible. Women, in particular, need to know about the women who went before us. We need to feel the enthusiasm and spirit of visionaries in order to rekindle our own spirit. We need confirmation that life is greater and more significant than what we see around us.

One way to resist the materialist, bottom-line culture, then, is to set aside time to study the lives of women in our past. The word "study" may sound dull and boring, but the Latin root means "enthusiasm and zest," and that's what we're searching for. Our spirit is enlivened when we learn about the accomplishments of women in history.

My study of women in history inspired me to take an unconventional route in my work. After being a community-college administrator for twenty-five years, I left my full-time position to work on the issue of Voluntary Simplicity, organizing simplicity study circles, a participant-led, egalitarian form of adult education that comes to us from Sweden. In my book *The Circle of Simplicity*, I develop a step-by-step plan that allows people to start and run their own simplicity circles. I couldn't have done all of this without knowledge of and inspiration from women in the past—in my graduate work at Stanford, I had taken many women's history courses. I would get so excited about women's lives that I couldn't sleep at night.

That is how you will feel about the women in this book. Seeing the things they accomplished and the risks they took will fill you with energy and exhilaration. But *Lost Legacy* takes you further. It reveals the ideas and beliefs that motivated these women—the life and philosophy of Emanuel Swedenborg, eighteenth-century scientist and visionary. Knowing that the women in *Lost Legacy* studied Swedenborg's ideas will be affirming for those who already are familiar with him and exciting for those who are looking for new paths to explore.

I am part of the latter group, for I only recently became acquainted with Swedenborg when I was asked to speak on the topic of simplicity at an annual Swedenborgian conference. It has been so exciting to discover his ideas—particularly his respect for women and the belief that women as well as men have the right and the duty to be "of use"—that we all have a need to make a difference in the fate of the world and the lives around us. And it has been particularly exciting for me to discover that many of the people who influenced my work were influenced by Swedenborg. For instance, one of my nineteenth-century role models, Margaret Fuller (who organized the equivalent of study circles in her program of "Conversations"), was influenced by Swedenborg. And again, the Transcendentalists, who influenced my work on simplicity, also studied Swedenborg. And I found many such examples in this book. One of the women in *Lost Legacy*, Harriot Hunt, was a figure I discussed in my dissertation on women in nontraditional careers. Another woman, Jesse Willcox Smith, illustrated a book that had a profound impact on me as I was growing up—Louisa May Alcott's *Little Women*. Mary Lathbury was the poet laureate of the nineteenth-century adult-education movement, the Chatauqua Institution. It was the Chautauqua movement that originally gave us the study circle, the method of adult education that has become my passion. (Representatives from Sweden visited the United States in the nineteenth century and took the methodology back where it is a major force in Swedish society.) Discovering these connections was somehow comforting to me—an affirmation that I am on the right path.

Reading this book helps us overcome the fact that our lives today are diminished by our culture's preoccupation with all that is trivial and shallow. It helps us remember that we are meant for something larger and more noble. The words and lives of the women in *Lost Legacy* will remind you that you are meant for something more. As you see these women dedicate themselves to the pursuit of their own paths—paths that not only changed the world around them but brought them ultimate satisfaction—you will be inspired to set out on your own journey. How wonderful to be able to say about your own work what Harriot Hunt said about hers when she realized how profoundly she was influenced by Swedenborg: "My profession assumed a magical power over me. . . . I had found the philosopher's stone, the elixir of life."

ACKNOWLEDGMENTS

❦

THE ORIGINAL IDEA for this book came from the collaboration of Alice Blackmer Skinner and Jane Williams-Hogan. Alice Skinner was also instrumental in acquiring funding for this project. A grant to the Swedenborg Foundation from the legacy of Lydia S. Rotch is acknowledged with deep gratitude.

John Hitchcock began the compilation of research provided by Louise Woofenden and Kira Gartner. Louise Woofenden contributed to the essays of Lydia Maria Child, Anna Cora Mowatt, and Jesse Willcox Smith. Susan Flagg Poole researched and wrote the essays for Harriot Hunt, Sarah Orne Jewett, Lydia Fuller Dickenson, Ednah Silver, Mary Lathbury, Selma Ware Paine, and Ellen Spencer Mussey. Mary Lou Bertucci, Donald Rose, George Dole, Robert Kirven, Alice Skinner, and Carol Lawson also offered valuable suggestions. Lucia Blackwell contributed to the early stages of the manuscript. Mathias Oppersdorf assisted in the photography, and Larry Conant provided some of the biographical information.

The complete essays of the Swedenborgian women who attended the World's Parliament of Religion in 1893 and Religious Congresses can be found in the *New Jerusalem in the World's Religious Congresses of 1893*, edited by L. P. Mercer and *Round Table Talks in Connection with New-Church Congress, 1893*, edited by A. E. Scammon, M. Burton, A. N. Waterman, and Clara Louise Burnham.

INTRODUCTION

by Susan Paine Flagg Poole

PLAYING ENDLESSLY in her family attic, a young girl dresses up in her ancestors' clothing. She adorns herself in a long black dress, a feathered hat, ivory gloves, and narrow, black-buttoned shoes. She admires her transformation before a gilded mirror. With a boned corset poking into her ribs and stiff lace scratching her skin, she imagines her great-grandmother attending tea parties and church socials. Her transformation is not just superficial; she also experiences an inner transformation. She is transported into another time and place. She feels a deep connection to another reality—a world of horse and buggies on cobblestone roads, piano music and singing in a rose-colored parlor, and oil lanterns flickering in the night; a day of chamber pots, wash boards, water pumps, handmade clothing, embroidered samplers, heavy irons, oxen, ploughs, and plain hard work—the realities of nineteenth-century America.

Time passes and the clothes in the dusty attic age and fray. The girl becomes a woman, a wife, a mother; her own daughter adorns herself with costume jewelry and period clothes from her grandmother's attic. She feels the magic of another time, another place. Singing songs from the Gay Nineties, she makes paper dolls, picks berries, bakes pies, and eats gingerbread cookies with her mother and grandmother.

The past touches the future in my childhood home. I am the young girl, the woman, the mother, and grandmother. My mother's life shines on my daughter. In this ancestral home, family portraits, journals and letters, stamps and coins, lace and linens, guns and swords, dishes and dolls elicit memories. Words, written in centuries past, come to life.

While looking through mementos of the past, one particular family book intrigued me: *The Discovery of a Grandmother: Glimpses into the Homes and Lives of Eight Generations of an Ipswich-Paine Family*. This book tells of the excitement my ancestors felt when they first explored the theological works of Emanuel Swedenborg, the noted eighteenth-century scientist and visionary.

Since the early 1800s, my relatives have read Swedenborg's works. They found comfort in the idea of a loving, merciful God who includes all people in the divine plan for humanity. Energized by the emphasis Swedenborg placed on leading a useful life and excited to learn about the inner sense of Scripture, they further explored his writing. My ancestors appreciated Swedenborg's descriptions of heaven and hell and saw the relevance of his ideas to their own lives. They wanted to view themselves as spiritual beings who would transcend their physical existence and continue the process of growth and development in a spiritual world. According to this philosopher and theologian, the purpose of existence was "to make an angelic heaven of the human race." With idealistic views and strong beliefs in eternal life, most of my ancestors tried to live with good intent and purpose.

My rich spiritual heritage is not unlike that of many other Swedenborgian families whose roots began in another religious tradition and then gradually turned to Swedenborgianism in nineteenth-century America. My family tree speaks, to some degree, to the gradual development of Swedenborgianism in this country. The story of the Paine family is unique, but their basic spiritual beliefs are similar.

My great-great grandparents, Abiel Ware Paine and Albert Paine, co-founders of the first Congregational Church in Winslow, Maine, raised eight children and accepted Swedenborg's concepts. Their son, Albert Paine, a prominent attorney, married Mary Hale, a Swedenborgian musician, formed a Swedenborgian study group, and raised a family in Bangor, Maine. Albert and Mary's daughter, Selma Ware Paine, educator and writer, represented Swedenborgians at the World's Parliament of Religions, held in 1893 in conjunction with the Chicago World's Fair. Timothy Otis Paine, Hebrew scholar, professor of Asian languages, poet, and notable Swedenborgian minister, married Agnes Howard, Swedenborgian writer and musician. Their children, grandchildren, and other descendants became Swedenborgian writers, artists, and musicians.

The Swedenborgian women featured in this book were writers, musicians, artists, or activists, who also taught school, raised children, and participated in local and national reform movements. They also were active in movements for the abolition of slavery, women's rights, and health reform. They promoted personal, spiritual, social, and political freedom. Swedenborg's concepts of divine love and wisdom, spiritual regeneration, the afterlife, finding one's true path and leading a useful life provided these women with a firm theological and philosophical base for their life's work.

The women in this anthology are united not only in their Swedenborgian beliefs or interests, but also in their social or educational background. In the nineteenth century, with many professions off limits, most women had difficulty finding meaningful work outside the home; but in spite of this, some became notable authors, artists, or musicians. While many women valued their spiritual freedom, others did not feel free to express themselves fully in either social or political terms. Their church organizations were often slow to respond to their needs, but their theology sustained them. Social standing and financial status did not exclude upper-class women from personal tragedy and internal struggles; children, like Dr. Harriot Hunt's niece, often died at very young ages. Diseases ravaged entire communities, leaving families heart-broken and in disarray. In fact, half of the women in *Lost Legacy* fought long-term battles with tubercular, arthritic, or other persistent medical conditions. Their faith, beliefs, and practices helped them get through difficult times, and perhaps extended their lives.

The letters, essays, and articles in this collection were written by women who led active lives, shared their love and understanding with others, committed themselves to God and neighbor, and searched for the truth and freedom in a world where social and cultural restrictions were often intolerable. Rising above the limitations placed upon them as they sought to be and become who they were meant to be, these women were unconventional and feisty. As they speak in their own voices, various themes emerge that begin to show the subtle influences on their lives and on the culture of nineteenth-century America.

This book is divided into two parts. Part one highlights public figures who became members of the Swedenborgian Church or were dedicated readers of Swedenborg: Lydia Maria Child, Harriot Hunt, Anna Cora Ogden Mowatt, Sarah Orne Jewett, and Jessie Willcox Smith.

Child's life was dedicated to public anti-slavery work. Her letters moved people at the highest levels of state and national responsibility, and many of her novels shocked the nation. She spent her life writing letters, articles, and books to promote freedom for all people.

Harriot Hunt, a medical practitioner and an advocate for women's rights, paved the way for future doctors. Her visionary view of holistic health enabled her to heal the bodies and spirits of numerous nineteenth-century women.

Actress Anna Ogden Mowatt found strength from her faith as she challenged the social restrictions put on women of nineteenth-century America. Her belief in an afterlife gave her the courage to overcome the personal challenges of her life. In her living and acting, she experienced higher spiritual domains.

Sarah Orne Jewett's novels *Deephaven* and *The Country of the Pointed Firs*, her most noted work, show the importance of love and friendship in spiritual, psychological, and physical healing.

Jesse Willcox Smith found personal and financial freedom with the success that came with her art work and illustrations. She generously shared her resources with others. Through the use of light, color, and symbolism, she captured the personalities of the children in her art and illustrations. These women, influenced by Emanuel Swedenborg, have also influenced others with their life's work.

The second part of this work illuminates Sweden-borgian concepts through the words of women who are largely unknown today, yet they were known within their communities and organizations in nineteenth-century America. In the 1800s, few opportunities existed for these women, yet their words have been recorded for posterity in church journals or regional publications. These women also share an honored place in the history of the 1800s, particularly in the historic events of the last decade—they all participated in the momentous occasion of the World's Parliament of Religion. The issues of abolition, voting rights, and personal, social, and political freedom were foremost in their thoughts. The celebration of these woman, who expressed their beliefs and made a difference in their own communities and beyond, is part of the purpose in presenting this work.

As church or community representatives, like Selma Paine, many Swedenborgian women spoke or presented papers at the first World's Parliament of Religion, held in conjunction with the 1893 Chicago World's Fair. Lydia Fuller Dickenson, educator, spoke on the theme of love and freedom; Ednah Silver, writer, titled her paper "The Ministry of Gentleness;" Mary Lathbury's hymns and Ellen Spencer Mussey's wise words welcomed guests from around the world. The mission of the Parliament was to hear the religious views of others with absolute respect. The visions that women shared at the time of the Parliament reflected the issues at hand in the general population. Leaders from different denominations across the country, as well as representatives from Eastern religions, were invited to present their unique perspectives in a pluralistic atmosphere.

The papers from the World's Parliament clarify a Swedenborgian perspective on the balancing of love and wisdom, leading a life of use, growing spiritually, seeing the microcosm within the macrocosm, treating the spiritual condition as well as the physical, and understanding the symbolic relationship between the natural and spiritual realms. These nineteenth-century women were inspired by Swedenborg's writing because of the value he placed on the qualities of love and understanding in both genders. Traditionally, the idea of woman as a creator of ideas and a problem-solver had not been valued equally to her role as nurturer. Swedenborg's views affirmed that each person, regardless of gender or race, has the ability to love and to understand equally. Margaret Fuller, a prominent nineteenth-century feminist writer, describes the impact of Swedenborg's ideas in her influential book *Woman in the Nineteenth Century*:

> His [Swedenborg's] idea of woman is sufficiently large and noble to interpose no obstacle to her progress. His idea of marriage is consequently sufficient. Man and woman share an angelic ministry, the union is from one to one, permanent and pure. . . . The mind of Swedenborg appeals to the various nature of man and allows room for aesthetic culture and the free expression of energy.[1]

In *Lost Legacy: Inspiring Women of Nineteenth-Century America*, a social reformer, physician, actress, novelist, illustrator, educator, writer, lyricist, poet, and an attorney reveal the foundation of their beliefs and the source of inspiration for some of their work. Through letters, articles, essays, novels, music, and artwork, small pieces of a lost legacy begin to unfold.

NOTES

1 Margaret Fuller, *The Portable Margaret Fuller*, edited by Mary Kelley (New York: Penguin, 1994), 297.

ON HER OWN PATH

Lydia Maria Child

CHAPTER ONE

HUMAN FREEDOM
Lydia Maria Child

*It is an inviolable Divine law that [a person] shall be
in freedom; and that good and truth, or charity and
faith, shall be implanted in freedom, and never under
compulsion; for what is received in a state of compulsion does not remain but is dissipated.*

Emanuel Swedenborg, Arcana Coelestia 5854[1]

LYDIA MARIA CHILD (1802–1880), writer and abolitionist, inspired many women throughout the
nineteenth century to stand for their rights and
to acknowledge the rights of all human beings to live as
free men and women. Well-known nationally by the
mid-nineteenth century, Child had considerable political and social influence, achieved through her spirited
and purposeful writing.

Born Lydia Maria Francis on February 11, 1802, Child
was one of the earliest American woman novelists to attain financial independence through her own writings.
Driven by social concerns throughout her life, Child
began her professional career in 1824 with *Hobomok*, a
novel that focuses on the relationship between a white

woman and a Native American, a work that created
quite a stir. Her interests being quite diverse, Child
published a book on household management for women
of little financial means (containing the earliest known
reference to baked beans) and wrote the lyrics to the
popular song "Over the river and through the woods,
to Grandmother's house we go." In addition, she founded
the first American magazine for children, *Juvenile Mis-
cellany*.

Child had been reading the works of Emanuel
Swedenborg. Although in 1820 she wrote a letter to her
brother, Convers Francis, assuring him that he should
"not fear my becoming a Swedenborgian," she joined
the church organization in 1822.[2] Unfortunately, because she felt that the ministers were not taking a strong
enough stand against slavery in their sermons, she soon
became disgruntled with the leadership. Child could
not understand why many of the clergy did not become
more actively involved in social movements. In spite of
her feelings toward the church organization, the ideas of
Swedenborg permeated her thought and writings, and
she believed that the only true church organization is
one in which heads and hearts unite in working for the
welfare of the human race.

The topic of human freedom, which so influenced
Child's public career, stands out in Swedenborg's works,
where he casts the issue of human freedom in spiritual
terms:

A human being is an organ of life, and God alone is
life. God pours his life into the organ and all its parts,
as the sun pours its warmth into a tree and all its
parts. Further, God grants people a sense that the life

in them seems to be their own.... Our free choice results from the fact that we have a sense that the life
we enjoy belongs to us.

True Christian Religion 504:5

Since each man and woman partakes of the life of
God and has been granted freedom of choice, it stands
to reason that no human being can own another, since
all stand equal before God's eyes. In other works,
Swedenborg expressed an especial affinity for Africans,
a remarkable attitude for an eighteenth-century Euro-
pean. For example, Swedenborg believed that Africans
were more connected to their interior being and more
capable of thinking on a spiritual plane (*Arcana Coelestia*
2604). These particular Swedenborgian tenets held special attraction for Child, as well as the view that we
should all strive to lead a life of love, wisdom, and use,
which became the motto for Child's life.

In 1828, Lydia Maria Francis married David Lee
Child, a Boston attorney and Massachusetts legislator.
Through William Lloyd Garrison, an active abolitionist, the couple became more aware of the horrors of the
treatment of Africans in the slave states. In 1833, Child
published *An Appeal in Favor of that Class of Americans
Called Africans*, the first anti-slavery book published in
the United States. In this work she promoted emanci-
pation and an end to racial discrimination, using histor-
ical, political, economic, moral, and spiritual arguments
to show that Africans were intellectually and spiritually
equal to others. As seen in the following letter, Child was
diligently working for the anti-slavery cause early in the
nineteenth century:

[To an anti-slavery contributor, 1833] Your unex-
pected donation was most gratefully received, though
I was at first reluctant to take it, lest our amiable
young friend had directly or indirectly begged the
favor....

We have good encouragement of success in the
humble and unostentatious undertaking to which
you have contributed. The zeal of a few seems likely
to counterbalance the apathy of the many. Posterity
will marvel at the hardness of our prejudice on this
subject, as we marvel at the learned and conscientious
believers in the Salem witchcraft. So easy is it to see
the errors of past ages, so difficult to acknowledge
our own!

Letters, 12[3]

Child was determined to be one of the few who took
action against the horrors of slavery. In her view, which
parallels Swedenborg's beliefs, apathy was considered to
be a great sin. Swedenborg believed that people should
take their talents, skills, and loves, and put them into use.
Child used her skills as a writer to express clearly and
vividly her strong and well-thought-out views on freedom for all people. In 1841 Child became editor of *The
Anti-Slavery Standard* in New York. *The Standard* grew
strong under her guidance, and she continued to write
in a wide variety of areas, including her voluminous
personal correspondence, in which she held forth on
the injustice of slavery:

[To her brother, September 25, 1835] I believe the
world will be brought into a state of order through
manifold revolutions. Sometimes we may be tempted

to think it would have been better for us not to have been cast on these evil times; but this is a selfish consideration; we ought rather to rejoice that we have much to do as mediums in the regeneration of the world....

You ask me to be prudent, and I will be so, as far as is consistent with a sense of duty; but this will not be what the world calls prudent. Firmness is the virtue most needed in times of excitement. What consequence is it if a few individuals do sink to untimely and dishonored graves, if the progress of great principles is still onward? Perchance for this cause came we into the world.

I have examined the history of the slaves too thoroughly, and felt their wrongs too deeply, to be prudent in the worldly sense of the term. I know too well the cruel and wicked mockery contained in all the excuses and palliations of the system.

Selected Letters, 39

The Fugitive Slave Law, enacted in 1850, providing for the return of escaped slaves across state lines, caused another battle in the war for freedom. Child used her literary and persuasive skills to fight this law, working to gain freedom for a slave who had escaped to the North, but had been returned under this law.

[To a friend, 1860] You doubtless remember Thomas Sims, the fugitive slave, who was surrendered in Boston, in 1852. I saw a letter from him to his sister expressing an intense longing for his freedom, and I swore "by the Eternal"...that as Massachusetts had sent him into slavery, Massachusetts should bring him back. I resolved, also, that it should all be done with pro-slavery money . . . . I expected to have to write at least a hundred letters, and to have to station myself on the steps of the Statehouse this winter, to besiege people. Sims is a skilful [sic] mechanic and his master asks $1800 for him. A large sum for an abolitionist to get out of pro-slavery purses! But I got it! I got it! I got it! Hurrah! I had written only eighteen letters, when one gentleman promised to pay the whole sum provided I would not mention his name.

Letters 144–145

Personal Liberty Bills were the North's response to the Fugitive Slave Law. These bills provided jury trials for escaped slaves who were apprehended in states that had enacted such laws. The Personal Liberty Bill in Massachusetts was at the center of much controversy, and Child again waged eloquent war with her pen:

[To Hon. Lemuel Shaw, Chief Justice of the Massachusetts Supreme Court 1830–1860, January 3, 1861] By this mail I send you three pamphlets, for which I ask a candid perusal. With deep sadness I saw your respected and influential name signed to an address in favor of repealing the Personal Liberty Bill. I trust you will not deem me disrespectful if I ask whether you have reflected well on all the bearings of this important subject.... This mutual agreement between North and South to keep millions of fellow-beings in abject degradation and misery cannot possibly be right. No sophistry can make it appear so to hearts and minds not frozen or blinded by the influence of trade or politics.

If the common plea of the inferiority of the African race be true, that only adds meanness to our guilt; the magnanimous strong are ashamed to protect the weak. Then everybody knows that an immense proportion of American slaves are not black....They are the sons and daughters of our presidents, governors, judges, senators, and generals. The much vaunted Anglo-Saxon blood is coursing in their veins, through generations after generations....

What answer will enlightened reason give, if you ask whether free institutions in one part of the country can possibly survive continual compromises with despotism in another part? If the lowest person in the community is legally oppressed, is not the highest endangered thereby? And does not the process inevitably demoralize the people by taking away from law that which renders it sacred, namely equal and impartial justice? I again ask you, respectfully and earnestly, to read my pamphlets with candid attention.... I believe you to be an upright and kind man, and therefore infer that your heart and conscience are not in fault, but only the blinding influences of your social environment.

Selected Letters, 367–368

The issue of slavery was not the only political cause that Child supported. She was also devoted to establishing the rights of women and had the foresight and courage to live her life according to her beliefs. After publication of *An Appeal on Behalf of the Class of Americans Called Africans,* Child's popularity had plummeted. The financial loss sustained, combined with her husband's impractical business decisions, caused her to take the unprecedented step of separating her assets from her husband's, thus legally protecting herself in case his ventures might jeopardize her own holdings. Women, like Child, who were exposed to Swedenborg's broader, nontraditional ideas were developing a deeper awareness of the wide variety of roles they might have in their communities. The idea that God is "divine love and wisdom," that the divine nature consists of feminine and masculine qualities, and that masculine and feminine comprise each gender influenced their thinking. The feminine aspect of God was given equal dignity with the masculine. According to Swedenborg, the feminine may even be said to encompass the masculine, since the divine love (feminine) is the substance of all reality, while divine wisdom (masculine) provides the form. Child's expanded beliefs led her to question the restrictions placed upon women.

At the time Child wrote the following letter, American women were still battling for many basic legal rights, not only the right to vote, but the right to have control over their own legal and financial matters:

[To a male friend, February 24, 1856] David has signed my will and I have sealed it up and put it away. It excited my towering indignation to think it was necessary for him to sign it, and if you had been by, you would have made the matter worse by repeating your old manly "fling and twit" about married women being dead in the law. I was not indignant on my own account, for David respects the freedom of all women on principle, and mine in particular by reason of affection superadded. But I was indignant for womankind made chattels personal from the be-

ginning of time, perpetually insulted by literature,
law, and custom....

I have such a fire burning in my soul, that it seems
to me I could pour forth a stream of lava that would
bury all the respectable servilities, and all the mob
servilities, as deep as Pompeii, so that it would be an
enormous labor ever to dig up the skeletons of their
memories . . . . What a shame the women can't vote!
We'd carry our "Jessie" [Jessie Benton Fremont, author, and wife of the 1856 Republican presidential
candidate, John C. Fremont] into the White House
on our shoulders; wouldn't we? Never mind! Wait a
while! Woman stock is rising in the market. I shall not
live to see women vote; but I'll come and rap at the
ballot-box. Won't you? I never was bitten by politics
before, but such mighty issues are depending on this
election that I cannot be indifferent.

Selected Letters, 279

For several decades, Child wrote letters to everyone
she knew concerning the issues that grieved her the
most. In the next letter on the topic of women's rights,
Child subtly uses language to make the point that, while
slavery was oppression in the extreme, the withholding
of rights for women was also a form of oppression not
to be tolerated:

[To Charles Sumner, 1879] I have been often urged
to write to you on what is called the "Woman Question." Our republican ideas cannot be consistently
carried out while women are excluded from any
share in the government. I reduce the argument to
very simple elements. I pay taxes for property of my

own earning and saving, and I do not believe in "tax-ation without representation." As for representation by proxy, that savors too much of the plantation sys-tem, however kind the master may be. I am a human being, and every human being has a right to a voice in the laws which claim authority to tax, to imprison, or to hang a person. The exercise of rights always has a more salutary effect on character than the enjoyment of privileges. Any class of human beings to whom a position of perpetual subordination is assigned, how-ever much they may be petted and flattered, must in-evitably be dwarfed, morally and intellectually.

But I will not enlarge on the theme. For forty years I have keenly felt my limitations as a woman, and have submitted to them under perpetual and indig-nant protest. It is too late for the subject to be of much interest to me personally. I have walked in fetters all my pilgrimage, and now I have but little farther to go. But I see so clearly that domestic and public life would be so much ennobled by the perfect equality and companionship of men and women in all the departments of life, that I long to see it accomplished, for the order and well-being of the world.

Letters 207–208

In the last year of her active life, Child reflected on her spiritual growth. She had discovered that, by work-ing hard for what she knew to be morally right, she had made a difference. She could see that her active partic-ipation in speaking out on issues that were important to her had helped to create social change, as well as helped to enrich her own life.

[To a friend, 1880] The memory of the early Anti-Slavery days is very sacred to me. The Holy Spirit did actually descend upon men and women in tongues of flame. Political and theological prejudices and personal ambitions were forgotten in sympathy for the wrongs of the helpless, and in enthusiasm to keep the fire of freedom from being extinguished on our national altar.

All suppression of selfishness makes the moment great and mortals were never more sublimely forgetful of self than were the abolitionists in those early days, before the moral force which emanated from them had become available as a political power. Ah, my friend, that is the only true church organization, when heads and hearts unite in working for the welfare of the human race.

Selected Letters, 561–567

Notes

1 The number following a work by Swedenborg indicates a paragraph or section number, which are uniform in all editions, rather than a page number.

2 Lydia Maria Child, *Selected Letters, 1817–1880,* edited by Milton Meltzer (Amherst, Mass.: University of Massachusetts Press, 1982), 2. Further references to this edition will be cited in the text as "Selected Letters."

3 Lydia Maria Child, *Letters of Lydia Maria Child* (1883; rpt. Boston: AMS Press, Inc., 1971). Further references to this edition will be cited in the text as "Letters."

13

Harriot Kezia Hunt

UNITING BODY, MIND, AND SPIRIT

Harriot Kezia Hunt

*Health is a musical key-note, it is the point of rest,
or action—it is the C, the whole melody of life rests
upon it.... God enters by a private door to each
individual, and when each one recognizes the fact and
leaves the door open to holy influences, then harmony,
melody will sing sweet songs of encouragement and an
inspiration in chorus.*

Harriot Hunt, *Glances and Glimpses*[1]

ARRIOT KEZIA HUNT (1805–1875), physician and reformer, was born in Boston, Massachusetts, and was reared in the liberal religious tradition of Unitarianism. Early in her life, she developed an interest in medicine, propelled by her sister's lingering illness. The Hunt family had lost confidence in conventional doctors after her sister Sarah had been treated by blistering, mercurial ointments, leeches, and prussic acid for a long-term tubercular condition. The results were ineffective, and Sarah remained seriously ill until alternative methods were employed.

In 1833 the Hunts met the Motts, a couple from England known for treating the spiritual condition as well as physical ailments. The Hunt sisters studied and worked with them for a period of time, and after Sarah recovered, they went into their own medical practice in 1835. The sisters focused on preventative medicine, nursing care, diet, bathing, exercises, rest, and hygiene. Most of their patients were tired, lacked motivation, felt inadequate, or had psychosomatic symptoms; and the psychotherapy methods that they used brought back some measure of health. Sarah and Harriot discovered through the experiences of their patients that physical maladies often seemed to grow out of concealed sorrows. Like the Motts, they understood that sickness was not limited to a physical condition. Illness was also a matter of the spirit, or a conflict between the internal and external and was subject to spiritual as well as physical treatment.

In her autobiography, Harriot Hunt describes the early days of their medical practice:

> I remember vividly the earnestness—the enthusiasm—with which we received our first patients. To be sure, they came along very slowly; but every case that did come, was a new revelation—a new wonder—a new study in itself, and by itself. The need of freedom of action—diversity of treatment—was constantly felt by us. Very early in medical life we found ourselves differing from our teachers, and escaping from formal rules. We very soon learned not to trust too much to medication:—not but that we often saw it fully successful; but it did not meet our perception of the dignity of the human body. Anatomy had partially opened its treasures to me; and the wonderful

deposits from the blood to develop, perfect, and sustain the system, even the bony structure, filled my soul with reverent awe: for I never entered the medical life through physics, but through metaphysics.

Glances and Glimpses, 127

In 1840, Sarah married Edmund Wright, and Harriot's life was significantly altered; Sarah stopped actively practicing medicine with her. Harriot describes the new channels of life that opened for her when she ventured out on her own:

My medical life received a new illumination: my patients gave me a new inspiration: new elements of thought came to me, which after experience was to shape and confirm. I had thought myself individual before, but it had only been at times. I had been in love with my profession: this change deepened the feeling very much. Fears and anxieties as well as pleasures attend all new relations when they are entered on reverently and with courage. My mother seemed invested with renewed sacredness, and childhood became stronger in my heart. I had not lost a sister, but gained a brother; but yet there was a discipline to pass through. Who that has had an only sister married but can understand my feelings! My life had now assumed more distinctness—more identity. I knew I must now, in a great measure, act alone. There was a widowed feeling about me, which passed away somewhat in time; but it has never wholly left me. The word "we," spoken professionally, sometimes escapes me now!

Glances and Glimpses, 165–166

Sarah and Harriot continued to live under the same roof after Sarah's marriage, and they remained close throughout their lives, but the focus of their daily activities began to change when Sarah and her husband started a family. Harriot continued to practice medicine throughout New England and other areas of the country, and was constantly challenged by the suffering and disease experienced by women. She resolved to do something about women's condition, and became personally involved with many families.

Hunt faced her own losses with the same courage and optimism. In 1845 Sarah's little daughter "passed into the spiritual sphere," and although Harriot grieved deeply, she said, "the yearning of my soul seemed to be met in New Church [Swedenborgian] truths" (*Glances and Glimpses*, 196). She used her faith and beliefs to make ongoing discoveries about the body, mind, and spirit. Harriot began seriously to examine Swedenborg's doctrines in order to deepen her understanding about the relationship between healing the body and spirit. In the winter of 1846, after hearing Harvard Professor George Bush lecture on Swedenborg's philosophy, Hunt joined the Boston Swedenborgian Church. Her own thoughts about holistic healing were compatible with Swedenborg's concepts.

While working with her patients, Hunt always took the time to listen to their problems, so she could plan a course of action to heal the whole body, which also includes the thoughts and feelings of an individual. She always kept in mind Swedenborg's words, as she had read them in *Divine Providence* 282: "To heal the understanding alone, is to heal from without, …and therefore the healing of the understanding would be like a palliative

healing.... It is the will itself which must be healed."
The basis for a rational method of spiritual healing can
be found in Swedenborg's works, and Harriot Hunt
drew upon the insights found in them.

> My profession assumed a magical power over me,
> just in proportion as I recognized the material body
> as a *type* only of the spiritual. This great and beauti-
> ful truth I found fully elaborated in Swedenborg's
> *Animal Kingdom*, and whilst reading it recognized
> perceptions which had always influenced my med-
> ical practice, although they never had been defined
> or embodied in my mind before. Light emanated
> from that work, which invested anatomy and physi-
> ology with golden robes. Clouds of mist vanished,
> and a flood of light dazzled me at first, but my men-
> tal vision became stronger by use, and soft, mellow
> tints attracted me along. Analysis rather than synthe-
> sis had been my peculiar habit; thus interior things
> opened from the exterior. Heaps of facts, gathered
> during my medical life, assumed form; sores laid by
> in the memory came forth from their hiding-places,
> and order was evolved from chaos. Many truths were
> found to be centered in one. I shall be termed an en-
> thusiast by many, but it matters not—I had found the
> philosopher's stone, the elixir of life.
>
> *Glances and Glimpses,* 197–198

After reading Swedenborg's *Animal Kingdom*, she read
his works *Divine Love and Wisdom* and then *Divine Providence*. She reported in her autobiography, "As the beauty
and simplicity of these doctrines opened on my mind,"
my rationality found a home. . . ." For her, Swedenborg

represented a holistic way to look at the world. She wrote
of his influence on her life:

> Gratefully do I acknowledge the influence of Sweden-
> borg's writings upon my mind, and I would say to all
> who are afflicted with doubt, disquiet, distrust, or de-
> spair, read the Bible — Divine love and wisdom will
> guide and cheer you. His writings appeal to the sci-
> entific as well as to the religious, for it is a remark-
> able fact, that it was not until after his mind was richly
> stored with a knowledge of the sciences, that he re-
> ceived that spiritual illumination, which shed light
> and glory over all creation.
>
> *Glances and Glimpses,* 205

As her understanding about the natural and spiritual
condition grew, so did her powers of observation. She
found that she gained insight into a patient's physical
condition through better understanding her spiritual
condition. In her autobiography Hunt wrote, "The
more truthfully we live to the laws of nature, the more
we are prepared to entertain the idea of freedom in its
spiritual, moral, and civil application. This truth has held
good with my patients" (*Glances and Glimpses,* 130). The
discoveries Hunt made from observing the experience
of her patients also enabled her to open her mind to
other medical systems. One such alternative system was
homeopathy:

> Although I knew little of homeopathy, yet I well
> remember the respect I felt for the details of its prac-
> titioners; and even the different kinds of fright por-
> trayed seemed worthy of consideration. The varied

degrees of grief and sorrow were early observed by
me in my patients, and I felt the positive need of
moral remedies. Sleeplessness caused by home-sick-
ness and by fright, never suggested to my mind the
same remedial means, the need was perceived of more
attention to subtle agencies and emotional states.

Glances and Glimpses, 174

Homeopathy is a total psycho-physical regime based
on the doctrines of "similarity and of infinitesimals,"
where drugs are administered in extremely small dilu-
tions. The principle is that the specific drug given mim-
ics the symptoms of the illness and aids in the natural
healing of the body. Such principles were compatible
with Swedenborg's idea that the physiological body is
derived from the spiritual, which must be affected first
for healing to take place. Homeopathy was popular in
nineteenth-century America and challenged the conventional, mainstream allopathic medicine. Many, with
conditions similar to Sarah Hunt, died in hospitals as
doctors continued to use the questionable practices of
blistering, bleeding, and purging. Homeopathy was a vi-
able spiritual and medicinal alternative and was highly
successful for many people. Although Hunt did not directly practice homeopathy, her view of medicine forced
her to examine and respect all methods that worked for
her patients, including a belief in a greater power. In her
approach, the value of her patients' contributions to their
own healing was equally important to the treatment
programs she recommended, which often included
prayer, meditation, or other relaxation techniques. Hunt
wrote, "I believe in mysticism—in the power of the
voice, in the magic of a hushed or an excited tone, in

the pressure of a hand, in the glance of an eye, in the sur-
rounding sphere; and I am wonderstruck at its power,
and reverently heed its monitions, for it speaks of deep
responsibilities" (*Glances and Glimpses*, 357).

Throughout her autobiography, Hunt quotes passages
from Swedenborg that particularly spoke to her and gave
form to chaos. After reading the following passage from
Swedenborg's *Animal Kingdom*, she reported that her understanding became deeper:

> As from the soul, the mind's principle in the brain,
> the nerves and blood vessels permeate the bony
> framework and cuticular enveloping of the body, pro-
> ducing the human form with its wonderful exterior
> uses—so the will and understanding take upon them-
> selves form and permeate through all the windings
> of thought and affection and give the quality of life
>
> Quoted in *Glances and Glimpses,* 199

In 1847 and again in 1850, Hunt was refused admit-
tance to Harvard Medical School. The rejection letter
said, "that it is *inexpedient* to reconsider the vote of the
corporation" regarding her request to attend the lec-
tures at the Medical College. Hunt did not take the rejection lightly. She explains other reactions to her
rejection letter:

> It was really amusing to hear the indignation ex-
> pressed by my patients and others, when they heard
> of the reply to my letter—the subject of woman as
> physician was before the public—the conversation
> on this and kindred topics increased tenfold, and tea-
> tables and evening parties were made merry with

criticisms and raillery, about the grave and weighty reason assigned for the refusal.... That word *inexpedient* I had always abhorred—it is so shuffling, so shifting, so mean, so evasive, meaning from the one who uses it every thing to the one who hears it nothing—an apology for falsehood, a compromise of principle to eke out self-satisfaction. It had always been a little word in my lexicon, and it became still littler, when used by a medical conclave. Any kind of a reason might have been accepted, but this "inexpedient" aroused my risibles, my sarcasm, my indignation.

Glances and Glimpses, 218–219

After her rejection from Harvard Medical School, she continued to practice medicine and had a renewed commitment to women's causes. Even though Harvard did not honor her requests for admission and recognition, she was not forgotten by other medical schools. After years of practice and thousands of patients, who experienced healing from her methods, Hunt formally became recognized as one of the first great woman physicians in American history. In 1853, the Female Medical College of Philadelphia granted Harriot Hunt an honorary degree of Doctor of Medicine.

In addition to her accomplishments in the medical field, Hunt became well-known for her involvement with the women's suffrage movement and the anti-slavery movement. She developed long-lasting friendships with many women reformers of nineteenth-century America. When she traveled across the country to lecture at medical schools and women's events, she would be asked questions about her spiritual beliefs. In response to the frequent question, "What do you think of spiritual manifestations?" Hunt answered:

> I believe in spiritual manifestations, in those holy unseen influences which arrest us from the within, and the effect is seen on the outer. In those spiritual communings when the outward eye is bright, because the inner is illuminated—when the tones are rich and clear and full, for voices within are speaking—when the expression is lighted up by a spark within—the innermost shining through the outermost. But I know not yet what to say of those manifestations which close the outer senses, that a concentration of nervous power may stimulate the inner. If the message be delightful, why do not the features become illuminated? Those nervous twitches speak not of harmony—those morbid feelings tell not of order, those unnatural actions savor not of health. This is the dark side of spiritualism.
>
> *Glances and Glimpses,* 356–357

Hunt was also grounded in rational thought and practical application of spiritual concepts. The issues of freedom, justice, and equality were constantly in her thoughts. She took concrete steps to promote social and political reform and actively protested when her rights were denied. By 1856 Hunt had earned a wide reputation for refusing to pay her taxes without representation. Her letters of protest were published in virtually every newspaper in the country, and politicians began to take notice. In an extract from one letter of protest, she complains:

Even drunkards, felons, idiots, or lunatics of men, may still enjoy that right of voting, to which not woman, however large the amount of taxes she pays, however respectable her character, or useful her life, can ever attain. Wherein, your remonstrant would inquire, is the justice, equality, or wisdom of this?

Glances and Glimpses, 294

Hunt dedicated her life to the health profession, and at the same time continued to promote freedom for all people, regardless of their sex, color, or class. Whether or not her patients could pay for her services, they were all treated equally. Hunt valued the life of the spirit, as well as the mind, and she was guided by strong spiritual principles. Through years of dedication and hard work, Harriot Kezia Hunt prepared the way for the first generation of women medical graduates of the 1850s and 1860s and was an inspiration to the other reformers who were paving the way in other fields of employment. In rediscovering this remarkable health practitioner, the successful techniques that she used to heal the mind, body, and spirit might also be revived.

NOTES

1 Harriot K. Hunt, *Glances and Glimpses: Or Fifty Years Social, including Twenty Years Professional Life* (Boston: Jewett and Company, 1856), 226–227. Further references to this work will be cited within the text.

Anna Cora Mowatt

NATURAL AND SPIRITUAL DIMENSIONS

Anna Cora Mowatt

*Some, therefore, have imagined the spiritual to be like
a bird flying above the air in an ether to which the
sight of the eye does not reach; when yet it is like a bird
of paradise which flies near the eye, even touching the
pupil with its beautiful wings and longing to be seen.*

Emanuel Swedenborg
Divine Love and Wisdom 27:374

ANNA CORA OGDEN MOWATT RICHIE (1819–1870),
author and actress, was born in Bordeaux,
France, where her father had been working for
several French exporting firms. The family moved to
New York City when she was six, and eventually grew
to a family of fourteen. At an early age, Anna, also called
"Lily," was encouraged to explore her love of poetry
and to develop her natural talents, which included
dramatization. Anna was an avid reader and frequently
performed for her large family.

In 1834 at the young age of fifteen, Anna eloped with
James Mowatt, a prosperous New York attorney thir-

teen years her senior. At first, her life was stable and secure, but within a few years of their marriage, she developed symptoms of tuberculosis and was encouraged
to rest and recuperate in Germany. While she started to
recover from her illness, her husband's health started to
decline. After consulting with Dr. Samuel Hahnemann,
founder of homeopathy, Mowatt's health was temporar-
ily restored. Due to James' financial speculation, the
Mowatts also had serious financial difficulties, so Anna
began to do public poetry readings to help support them.
Some of their friends were horrified when she made a
profit from reading poetry and performing in public,
then considered inappropriate for a proper woman.

With the stress from continuing health problems, the
Mowatts began to explore alternative approaches to
healing. In nineteenth-century America, many unusual
practices were being used to battle health problems; one
was the use of hypnotism. Anna began to use hypnotism
to treat her respiratory condition. While in a trance, she
would carry on long religious conversations with her
husband. When she awoke from the hypnotized state,
she did not remember anything, but said that she was
aware of a higher dimension. Through the use of hypnotism (also called mesmerism), she experienced altered
states of consciousness. Anna was put into a somnam-
bulic state hundreds of times to subdue her life-threat-
ening cough. A few people witnessed what she said
when she was hypnotized, and one friend told her about
what he had observed:

Frequently you would talk, like one inspired, of spiritual realities and the meaning of life. What in your

waking state was faith, seemed to be sight in you som-
nambulic. It was no longer a speculation, or even a belief, that there was a life after death, but a knowledge,
far more confident and assured than that which we
usually entertain, on going to bed, that we shall wake
in the morning.[1]

Some people began telling Mowatt that she must
have read Emanuel Swedenborg's works because of
what she was reporting when she was hypnotized. She
had not yet read Swedenborg, but soon began to inves-
tigate his ideas. She found that Swedenborg's descriptions of the inner states were similar to the experiences
some people had while mesmerized and could serve as
a guide to higher spiritual domains. Mowatt realized she
was living on two levels—the natural and the spiritual.
In her autobiography, she describes her experience:

> I read with avidity; and involuntarily, from an inter-
> nal conviction, as it were, accepted the doctrines. I
> never had a doubt to combat. Sometimes it seemed
> to me as though I had known all that was there re-
> vealed—believed it all before—only I had never de-
> liberately thought on the subject.
>   With the full acceptance of New Church doctrines
> came "the cheerful faith, that all which we behold is
> full of blessings." All things in life wore a different as-
> pect. I realized that the things which befall us in time
> had no true importance except as they regarded eter-
> nity. Whatever we received from above was good,
> whether it came in the shape of prosperity or mis-
> fortune, for it was but a means to fit us for our future

states. It became easy to perceive that the most trivial of "our daily joys and pains advance to a divine
significance." Life's trials lost all their bitterness.

Autobiography of an Actress, 169–170

Shortly after discovering Swedenborg's writings, the
Mowatts joined a Swedenborgian Church in New York.
They found that their new beliefs provided a source for
strength and hope, and they continued to be active in
the church throughout their lives. With her new beliefs,
Anna was no longer worried about what would happen
after she died. She lost all fear of death and was able to
live with new enthusiasm. With a revived sense of freedom and renewed zest for living, Anna took three children from the slums of New York under her angel wing.

The fame of Mowatt's poetry readings grew steadily
throughout the 1840s. Dr. Harriot Hunt, nineteenth-
century medical practitioner, writes about Mowatt's
magnetic personality in her own autobiography, *Glances
and Glimpses:*

In October, 1841, we went to the readings by Anna
Cora Mowatt, at the Masonic Temple. It was her first
appearance here. I remember my delight and wonder. She magnetized her audience. I was immediately
drawn to her. I felt a newness in my own life, and a
response to hers—and I only asked that every women
who went forth might be as well prepared as she was.
A pleasant intimacy with this noble, gifted woman,
in after years, proved to me how much can be accomplished in any profession when the ideal is high.
I shall have occasion to speak of her again in connection with the stage, and sustain my position, that

every woman, as well as man, should be considered as the most proper judge of their own sphere;— capacity, fitness, and attraction being the tests, instead of public opinion.

Glances and Glimpses, 168–169

Throughout the 1840s, Mowatt experienced the most productive period of her life. In 1845 she wrote a very successful play called *Fashion, or Life in New York,* a satire on contemporary high life. Shortly after this work was published, she started acting on the New York stage, although a woman had to be courageous to take on the acting profession because the theater was often seen as a house for sin and evil, and the social ramifications could be severe. Because of her remarkable style, modulated voice, and energized interpretations, Mowatt successfully portrayed Shakespeare's Juliet, Desdemona, Beatrice, Viola, and Rosalind, as well as many other heroines.

In *Five Smooth Stones,* a Swedenborgian publication for children, Louise Woofenden describes how Mowatt's life changed after she gained new strength and energy:

Anna's career blossomed. She began writing plays, and at the urging of professionals in the theater, became an actress and leading lady. What a gruelling profession it was then! Playing night after night, sometimes in one play after another; rehearsing for hours in the daytime and performing until late at night. Hours of uncomfortable train and stage coach rides. Living in hotel after hotel. Seasickness on the long voyages to England and the Continent. Working, working. Miraculously, Anna's health, instead of giving way, grew better and better. She had found something she

Anna Cora Mowatt as Beatrice

loved to do, and in doing it received energy from above. She became one of America's greatest actresses, praised by critics on both sides of the ocean.

At the height of her career, in 1851, Anna Mowatt lost her husband. His belief in the future life enabled him to die peacefully, though Anna was saddened by the fact that she was not with him when he went.

Her own religious beliefs were also strong. At one point, in a British theater, everyone was in mourning for Queen Adelaide, wife of William IV of England. At the performance one night, the entire cast was required to wear black. Anna refused. Death to her was awakening to a higher life. Black symbolized only death. When the curtain rose, the whole audience was clothed in black, and all the cast, except Anna, who looked lovely in a white crepe dress with white streamers.[2]

In 1854, Anna Mowatt married William Ritchie, editor of the *Richmond Enquirer*. Richie was also from a prominent Virginian family. *The New York Herald* published the Swedenborgian Church service verbatim and reported that "from bridesmaids and lace to champagne for two thousand people," everyone agreed that "there had never been a wedding like it." After the wedding, the Richies moved to Richmond, Virginia, where Anna soon began to struggle with bouts of bronchitis and pneumonia. Though ill at times, Anna became active in the movement to acquire Mount Vernon for a national shrine, and she continued to be productive. In 1856, she published *Mimic Life*, a collection of three tales about her theatrical life and, in 1857, a novel titled *Twin Roses*.

Anna spent the summers in New England, visiting family and friends. With her father and sisters, she could more easily express her Swedenborgian faith. People in the South were suspicious of her religion, and even her husband was becoming impatient with her beliefs, which were quite different from his own and incompatible with the mores of his society. Because of the hostility toward her beliefs, Anna rarely discussed religion with her new friends and soon began to avoid talking about it even with her own husband. This reluctance to share her innermost beliefs eventually led to their separation. When the Civil War began, Anna, who believed in freedom and felt that slavery should end, left her husband and returned to the northern states.

In 1860 Samuel Ogden, Anna's beloved father, died. She gained solace from her religion, but it was the greatest loss she experienced since the death of her first husband. Shortly after her father's death, she heard of her sister's illness, withdrew her money from the bank, and, sailed to France to be with her.

During the winter of 1861, Anna developed a friendship with Douglas Home, an extraordinary spiritualist. Anna was interested in spiritualism because it seemed to confirm Swedenborg's concept of the materiality of spirits. Although Swedenborg and the Swedenborgian Church never encouraged deliberate communication with spirits from other worlds, Anna was curious. With her father and James Mowatt both in the spiritual world, she wanted to explore higher realms.

After several years of traveling between Europe and America, Anna's health became worse. Her tubercular condition worsened, and she coughed incessantly. Living a life of inner and outer adventure, she spent the last two years of her life in England where she died of tuberculosis at the age of fifty.

Anna Cora Mowatt Richie, an actress famous in nineteenth-century America, is virtually unknown today; however, her comic play *Fashion* was revived in New York in 1924 and 1959 and is still performed in college and local theaters.

NOTES

1 Anna Cora Mowatt [Ritchie], *Autobiography of an Actress: Or Eight Years on the Stage* (Boston: Ticknor, Reed, and Fields, 1853), 178. All further references to this work will be cited in the text.

2 Louise Woofenden, "Famous Readers of Swedenborg: Anna Ogden Mowatt," *Five Smooth Stones* (September 1985): 11–12.

Sarah Orne Jewett

CHAPTER FOUR

THE PRESENCE OF OTHER WORLDS
Sarah Orne Jewett

*The whole natural world corresponds to the spiritual
world; not only the natural world in general, but also
every particular part thereof. The world of nature
comes forth and subsists from the spiritual world, just
as an effect does from its efficient cause.*

Emanuel Swedenborg
Divine Love and Wisdom 134

SARAH ORNE JEWETT (1849–1909), author, was born
in South Berwick, Maine. Her grandfather, Dr.
William Perry, a notable nineteenth-century
surgeon, and her father, also a doctor, deeply influenced
her. Although she was often ill as a young child, Sarah's
father took her with him when he visited his patients.
She absorbed everything about the people, the region,
the homes, and the landscapes in her surroundings. Her
family, community, and spiritual beliefs became a rich
source of inspiration and information for her. The
themes, characters, and settings of her novels meticu-
lously reflect these experiences.

In 1872 Jewett met Theophilus Parsons, a Harvard law
professor and leader of the Swedenborgian New Church.

Parsons' Swedenborgian beliefs had a profound impact on her, and she became very attracted to Swedenborg's writings. During the formative years of her own writing, Jewett's friendship with Parsons blossomed. They wrote frequently to one another, and she began to seriously explore Swedenborg's ideas on the relationship between the natural and spiritual worlds. Swedenborg discussed the wonders that can be found in nature, as illustrated in this excerpt from his work *Rational Psychology*:

> In the human body Nature has gathered together and poured forth the whole of her art and science....The longer one dwells on them, the more numerous are the marvels and hidden mysteries brought to light; and though thrice the age of Nestor was his, yet other mysteries remain. . . . Nature is an abyss, as it were, and nought remains but *amazement*.

In addition to introducing Jewett to Swedenborg's books, Parson's also encouraged her to write with passion and commitment as she developed the characters within her novel. In *Deephaven* (1877), her first full-length novel, Jewett integrates her ideas into the thoughts of her imaginary characters as she tells the story of two city girls coming to a small Maine village for the summer. One evening, characters Kate and Helen sit by the fire and discuss the people they have met during their summer visit. The importance of nature in their lives and the closeness of other realities come to light in their discussions:

> "I wonder," said I, "why it is that one hears so much more of such things [the mystery of the next world]

from simple country people. They believe in dreams, and they have a kind of fetishism, and believe so heartily in supernatural causes. I suppose nothing could shake Mrs. Patton's faith in warnings. There is no end of absurdity in it, and yet there is one side of such lives for which one cannot help having reverence; they live so much nearer to nature than people who are in cities, and there is a soberness about country people oftentimes that one cannot help noticing. I wonder if they are unconsciously awed by the strength and purpose in the world about them, and the mysterious creative power which is at work with them on their familiar farms. In their simple life they take their instincts for truths, and perhaps they are not always so far wrong as we imagine. Because they are so instinctive and unreasoning they may have a more complete sympathy with Nature, and may hear her voices when wiser ears are deaf. They have much in common, after all, with the plants which grow up out of the ground and the wild creatures which depend upon their instincts wholly."

"I think," said Kate, "that the more one lives out of doors the more personality there seems to be in what we call inanimate things. The strength of the hills and the voice of the waves are no longer only grand poetical sentences, but an expression of something real, and more and more one finds God himself in the world, and believes that we may read the thoughts that He writes for us in the book of Nature."[1]

In her novels, Jewett emphasizes the strength of local Maine women, their integrity, and their way of living as they work to become independent and fulfilled. Her belief in a personal God whose love for humanity is expressed through love, understanding, and responsibility is a belief that is expressed by many of her characters. Caring for the neighbor, using nature to learn about ourselves and others, and staying in touch with a force that is greater than ourselves are themes that surface frequently in Jewett's work. Believing in a world beyond, opening oneself to a divine intelligence, acting with kindness, and sharing mutual responsibility with others are some values that Jewett emphasizes. She often describes the small community within the larger one, shedding light on the concept of the microcosm reflected in the macrocosm, a concept that Swedenborg brings to an intimate, personal level. In *Apocalypse Explained* 969, he writes, "A person is a microcosm,...an image of the world."

Literary scholar Paula Blanchard describes another Swedenborgian view that is reflected in D*eephaven*:

> There is one thematic thread in *Deephaven* that we can probably trace directly to Swedenborg, and that is the belief in the transmigration of consciousness. As Parsons explained it, "the soul while in the material body makes that body live, and through it perceives the things of this material world." In death, "we, in our spiritual body, rise from the material body." But the spiritual world to which we pass is only a purged replica of the one we have left. In such a universe, it does not seem unlikely that spirits might communicate not only between worlds but within the material world.[2]

Jewett's belief in a divine purpose for life and an existence after this life found creative expression through her colorful characters. In *Deephaven*, Captain Sands uses an illustration from nature to make his point:

> We've got some faculty or other that we don't know much about. We've got some way of sending our thought like a bullet goes out of a gun and it hits. We don't know nothing except what we see. And some folks is scared, and some more thinks it is all nonsense and laughs. But there's something we haven't got that hang of. It makes me think o' them little black polliwogs that turns into frogs in the fresh-water puddles in the ma'sh. There's a time before their tails drop off and their legs have sprouted out, when they don't get any use o' their legs, and I dare say they're in their way consider'ble; but after they get to be frogs they find out what they're for without no kind of trouble. I guess we shall turn these fac'lties to account some time or 'nother. Seems to me, though, that we might depend on 'em now more than we do.
>
> *Deephaven,* 96–97

In *Heaven and Hell* 461, Swedenborg uses his own spiritual experiences to elucidate the transition from one kind of existence to another:

> [W]hen a person crosses from one life to the other, . . . it is as though he or she had gone from one place to another and had taken . . . all the things possessed . . . as a person. . . . all the things he or she has heard, seen, read, learned, or thought in the world from earliest infancy right to the last moment of life.

In 1878 Jewett's father "passed from one life to the other," and she experienced a deep loss after his death. Her father's suggestion "to not write *about* things, but to write about things just as they are" was valuable advice to her. She carried these words with her for the rest of her life. Shortly after losing her father, Jewett began to develop a close friendship with writer Annie Adams Fields. When Annie's husband, James Fields, died, the close relationship of Sarah and Annie filled a deep need for both women. As they socialized with other poets, musicians, artists, and writers, Jewett and Fields became intimate friends and companions. For several months each year, they lived together in Boston and traveled extensively. When they were apart, they frequently corresponded, sharing literary thoughts, health remedies, and the weekly news within their own communities. Sarah wrote a letter to Annie on June 24, 1883, stating:

> I wonder how far you have gotten in the Swedenborg book? I keep a sense of it under everything else. How such a bit of foundation lifts up all one's other thoughts together, and makes us feel as if we really stood higher and could see more of the world. I am going to hunt up some of the smaller books of extracts, etc., that Professor Parsons gave me.[3]

Jewett and Fields wrote letters, articles, and shorter pieces for a variety of magazines and literary journals; however, Jewett became the more passionate writer. In a 1908 letter to Willa Cather, she passed on her father's sentiments to another promising writer:

> You must write to the human heart, the great con-

sciousness that all humanity goes to make up. Otherwise what might be strength in a writer is only crudeness, and what might be insight is only observation; sentiment falls to sentimentality—you can write about life, but never write life itself. And to write and work on this level, we must live on it—we must at least recognize it and defer to it at every step.

Letters, 249

In *The Country of the Pointed Firs* (1896), Jewett's best-known novel, she again heeds to the advice of her father and writes about what she knows best: the rural life and people of coastal Maine. In this novel, an herb gatherer keeps alive the wisdom of the past through homeopathic remedies, an area of great interest to many Swedenborgians in nineteenth-century America. In the first scene of the novel, Jewett captured the essence of the main character, Mrs. Todd, as she describes her distributing remedies from her herb garden:

At one side of this herb plot were other growths of a rustic pharmacopoeia, great treasures and rarities among the commoner herbs. There were some strange and pungent odors that roused a dim sense and remembrance of something in the forgotten past. Some of these might once have belonged to sacred and mystic rites, and have had some occult knowledge handed with them down the centuries.... It may not have been only the common ails of humanity with which she tried to cope; it seemed sometimes as if love and hate and jealousy and adverse winds at sea might also find their proper remedies among the curious wild-looking plants in Mrs. Todd's garden.

43

In this novel, disease is seen as also being a matter of the spirit, or a conflict between the internal and external. Disease was subject to spiritual treatment, as well as physical treatment. This theme also was influenced by Jewett's reading of Swedenborg; for example, Swedenborg wrote in *Divine Providence* 282 that "to heal the understanding alone is to heal from without. The will itself needs to be healed." These thoughts are reflected in the discussions of Jewett's characters.

In *Notable Women: A Biographical Dictionary*, Warner Bertoff summarized Jewett's inner life as follows:

> Of her own thought and spirit her letters are the best evidence. She does not seem to have been profoundly religious, although through her friendship with Prof. Theophilus Parsons of the Harvard Law School, and leader of the New Church, she was attracted to Swedenborgianism, keeping as she said, "a sense of it under everything else"; she found scarcely less comfort in the flowers of her own garden. A latent assurance that the "mysterious moment of death" would prove "a moment of waking" did not reduce her keen consciousness of "all that lay this side the boundary."[4]

In 1901, after a life filled with many literary achievements, including the publication of eighteen novels, Jewett was granted a literature degree from Bowdoin College in Brunswick, Maine. Unfortunately, only one year later, on her fifty-third birthday, Jewett sustained a serious injury after being thrown from her carriage, an injury from which she never fully recovered. After this accident, she stayed closer to home, but continued to write. In 1909, she suffered a paralyzing stroke and died several weeks later at her home in South Berwick, Maine.

Jewett's strong belief in an afterlife helped her through her many losses, including the last physically challenging years of her own life. Sarah Orne Jewett's personal belief in a God whose care for humanity is expressed through love, understanding, and responsibility was evident not only in many of her characters, but also in her own life. Her strength, integrity, and personality find expression throughout her creative work.

NOTES

1 Sarah Orne Jewett, *Novels and Stories: Deephaven, A Country Doctor, The Country of the Pointed Firs, Dunnet Landing Stories, Selected Stories and Sketches* (New York: The Library of America, 1994), 103. All further references to Jewett's novels are taken from this collection and will be citied in the text.

2 Paula Blanchard, *Sarah Orne Jewett: Her World and Her Work* (Reading, Massachusetts: Addison-Wesley Publishing Company, 1994), 95–96.

3 Sarah Orne Jewett, *Letters of Sarah Orne Jewett*, edited by Annie Fields (Boston: Houghton, Mifflin, 1911), 21–22. Further references to Jewett's letters are taken from this work and will be cited in the text.

4 Warner Bertoff, "Sarah Orne Jewett," in *Notable American Women: A Biographical Dictionary*, vol. 2, edited by Edward T. James, et al (Cambridge: Harvard University Press, 1971), 276.

Jesse Willcox Smith

REFLECTIONS OF THE INNER LIFE

Jesse Willcox Smith

*There are splendid palaces in the spiritual heaven,
where everything glows from within with precious
stones, and with ornaments so exquisitely formed that
they cannot be reproduced by any painting on earth.*
Emanuel Swedenborg, *Apocalypse Explained* 831:6

JESSIE WILLCOX SMITH (1863–1935), a visual artist
and career illustrator, was born in Philadelphia,
Pennsylvania, during the Civil War. As a young
adult, she planned to teach school, which was one of
the few career choices in nineteenth-century America
that was considered appropriate for young women.
Although Smith had a deep love for children and teaching, she abandoned her plans when she discovered she
had a talent for drawing after taking an art class with a
friend, and entered the School of Design for Women in
Philadelphia.

In the fall of 1885, Smith joined the Pennsylvania
Academy of the Fine Arts and studied under Thomas
Eakins. Eakins insisted on equal rights for his women
students, and with his guidance and support, Smith

began to develop the skills that she would need to survive as a woman in the art world. She soon earned the reputation for being a "jack-of-all-trades." The working world was not friendly and open to women artists, but with her reputation for doing outstanding work, she was starting to be noticed.

In June of 1888, Smith was graduated from the Fine Arts Academy and began working as a freelance illustrator, then accepted a job working in the advertising department at *The Ladies' Home Journal* in Philadelphia. She also did drawings for *St. Nicholas* magazine, but her style did not fully develop until she began her work under the guidance of Howard Pyle.

In 1894, Smith was accepted into Drexel University as a student of Howard Pyle, who was one of the most influential art teachers in nineteenth-century America. Pyle's mother, a member of the Swedenborgian Church in Wilmington, Delaware, brought Howard to church on Sundays, exposing him to Swedenborgian concepts at an early age. The idea of correspondences, or symbolic representations, appealed to Pyle, and also stimulated the minds of many other artists. Using symbolic language, everything in the natural world has a spiritual correspondence. Swedenborg's concepts also influenced Pyle's beliefs about the spiritual world, and he read many selections from Swedenborg's works to his students. The vivid visual images inspired them and helped them look beneath the surface. With their "spiritual" eyes opened, they could see other possibilities for their lives and their work. Passages from Swedenborg spoke of the hills and mountains, gardens and flowers, and a spiritual world that exists simultaneously with the natural world. Swedenborg created colorful images that helped the artists bring out the beauties of nature in their work. While studying with Pyle, Smith used the imagery found in Swedenborg as an inspiration for her painting and for her life. She thought about higher things, which elevated her thoughts, and consequently brought more depth and meaning into her paintings.

Smith became a member of the Swedenborgian Church to further explore her faith and her life's work. When her studio was in Chestnut Hill in Philadelphia, she became involved with her friends and the activities at the church; but when she moved outside the city, it became difficult to get to Sunday services. Her reading of Swedenborg, however, continued to inspire and influence her.

At the time of her studying at Drexel, Pyle helped Smith find commissioned work, and her skill and confidence grew. After successfully completing two illustrated books on American Indian artifacts, Smith informed her publisher that she could also paint other subjects. She was asked to illustrate Louisa May Alcott's *Little Women*, which became one of her most famous works of art. With her remarkable ability to capture the innocent qualities and personality of young children, she never had difficulty finding work again.

Smith avoided using professional models and preferred to observe children playing in their natural environment before drawing them. She liked to illustrate children who were hearty, busy, and spirited. The illustrations depicted in *Little Women* demonstrate her wonderful ability to bring out the inner qualities of young people.

Determined to follow her own path, Smith was open to new adventures. She continued to study with Pyle at

Jesse Willcox Smith's cover for Little Women

Drexel, and while studying met a number of other artists interested in careers as illustrators. One of these artists, Elizabeth Shippen Green, also worked in the advertising department of *The Ladies' Home Journal*. Artist Violet Oakley then came to Drexel to study with them, and Pyle observed the compatible styles of Smith and Oakley. The two women illustrated Henry Wadsworth Longfellow's *Evangeline* together. Jessie H. Dowd, another Pyle student, joined Oakley and Smith, and the three shared studio/living space. Shortly after, Elizabeth Shippen Green also came to live with them; later Henrietta Cozens joined the group of working artists, contributing to the household by managing the finances and enabling the others to focus on their work. Each artist ultimately became successful.

In 1902 Smith was awarded a bronze medal for her paintings at the International Exposition in Charleston, South Carolina. This award gave her national attention, which was important to the business side of her art career. More doors of opportunity opened.

Success led to financial freedom for Smith, as well as for her friends. With a secure financial situation, the artists were able to choose only the assignments that appealed to them. They were also able to finance their own projects: Smith and Green teamed to create a calendar called "The Child," featuring paintings of young children at play. The calendar was reprinted as a book called *The Book of the Child*.

After a period of time, the artists moved to a farmhouse and named it Cogslea (Cozens, Oakley, Green, and Smith). Cozens hired a cook, maids, and a gardener. When Smith's brother became ill, he came to live with the group, as did Smith's ailing sister, who was unable to care for her children. Smith took the children in and provided for them, as she did for the rest of her extended family. Her generosity of spirit and compassionate inner qualities were well known among her friends. Although Smith never married or had children, she cared for several adults, eleven children, and members of her own family, sharing her considerable gifts with others. She also donated posters, artwork, and her time to orphanages and numerous charities. "A Simple Faith Has Made America Great," painted for the 1919 Interchurch World Movement, is a fine example of her poster work.

By 1911, Smith was the most popular children's book illustrator of the time. Her work illuminated the pages of *Dream Blocks*, *A Child's Book of Old Verses*, *A Child's Book of Stories*, and other works; her illustrations had a dreamy yet realistic quality. The simplicity and innocence of a child's personality could be seen in her work, but she did not want her paintings to be too sentimental, so she carefully studied individual children at work and at play. Although Smith was in great demand and worked constantly, the death of Howard Pyle in 1911 brought sadness to her home. Pyle had brightened not only her art, but also her spirit.

After Pyle's death, Smith built a house near Cogslea and moved into the new home with her friends and relatives. Cozens, Oakley, Green, and Smith christened the home Cogshill. Continuing to work, Smith illustrated Charles Kingsley's *The Water Babies*, painted cover illustrations for *Good Housekeeping Magazine*, and illustrated many books. She occasionally went to the Art School in Philadelphia (now called the Philadelphia College of Art) to talk to the students about composition and style.

Poster art by Jesse Willcox Smith

In 1933 Smith's health began to fail, but accompanied by a nurse, she managed to travel to Europe, in spite of her impaired vision and difficulty walking. After this trip she continued to struggle with poor health for two more years, then succumbed to an inflamation of the heart and kidneys in 1935. One of the favorite stories told concerning Smith occurs at the time of her death:

> On the night of May 3, 1935, Edith Emerson, one of Smith's dearest friends, had a very alarming dream. She saw Smith, on her deathbed, suddenly rise and get dressed. She further saw Smith, despite her nurse's vehement objections, throw open the French windows leading to the outside gardens and softly disappear into the night. Emerson awoke and knew that her lifelong friend had died. An hour later she received a call confirming the news.[1]

At a memorial exhibit of Smith's works, held at the Pennsylvania Academy of the Fine Arts in 1936, Edith Emerson paid tribute to her friend Jesse Willcox Smith: "hers was a brave and generous mind, comprehending life with a large simplicity, free from all pettiness, and unfailingly kind." In addition to being remembered for her kindness, her love of children, and her gift of giving, the legacy of Smith's artwork continues to be appreciated in children's books, museums, and private collections around the world.

NOTES

1 Edward Nudelman, *Jesse Willcox Smith: American Illustrator* (Gretna, La: Pelican Publishing Company, 1990), 45.

PART TWO

IN HER OWN WORDS

Lydia Fuller Dickenson

GENUINE LOVE AND FREEDOM
Lydia Fuller Dickenson

*All freedom is a matter of love, to the point that love
and freedom are one thing. Everything we have that
brings us joy comes from our love,...[and our] joy
leads us along [just as] a river carries things along
with its current.*

Emanuel Swedenborg, *Divine Providence* 73:2

LYDIA FULLER DICKENSON (1828–1904), educator
and essayist, was born in Massachusetts in 1828.
In 1847 she married D. L. Dickenson in Cincin-
nati, Ohio, then moved to St. Louis, Missouri, where she
and her husband raised their family. Active in the
women's movement and the Fourierist social movement, she advanced the cause for personal, social, and
political freedom in many of her essays and articles.

The concepts of Emanuel Swedenborg and those of
Charles Fourier, the nineteenth-century French socialist, appealed to Dickenson. She saw a compatibility
between Swedenborg's writings on the natural and spiritual worlds and the Fourierist ideal of universal unity
and equality. Both philosophers were accepting of all

creeds and faiths that promoted good and truth for humanity.

Nineteenth-century women were particularly interested in Fourierist settlements because, in these communities, women shared equal legal and political status with men. Although many Swedenborgians were generally attracted to Fourier's concepts, the Swedenborgian Church quickly parted ways with the movement over Fourier's socialist theories. Brook Farm, originally a transcendentalist community, whose mission was to create a miniature world in which each member could be fully developed, evolved into a Fourierist Phalanx in 1845. Swedenborgians were involved with this community for a short period.

For several decades, Dickenson promoted the works of philosopher and author Henry James, Sr. (1811–1882) —father of William James and Henry James, Jr., the novelist. She hosted literary gatherings to discuss his material. James wrote books that demonstrated his interest in Fourier and Swedenborg, citing Fourier's scientific insight and practical social science as complementing the concepts of Swedenborg. As Dickenson's understanding of the works of Swedenborg, Fourier, and James continued to deepen, she enlivened literary clubs and study groups with her insights. As many other educated, professional women of the nineteenth century, Dickenson found an outlet for her creativity and intellect through reading, writing, and public speaking. Indeed, publicly reading the works of James Sr. became one of her passions. Her natural teaching abilities and her willingness to engage in intellectual discourse earned her respect.

In 1893 Dickenson represented St. Louis Swedenborgian women as a delegate to the World's Parliament of Religions held in Chicago. Dickenson addressed Swedenborg's concept of divine love and wisdom and the masculine/feminine balance in the paper that she presented during the main session of the Parliament:

> To those who can accept it, sacred history satisfactorily answers the [woman's] question [of equality and freedom]. From this source we learn that He who made them in the beginning, made them male and female; that the creative bond between them is the bond of marriage admitting of no divorce because they are no longer two but one, being joined together by God Himself, that is creatively. In a relation of essential oneness, such as is contemplated here, there can of course be no subjection of one to the other, no separation between them. They are complementary to each other. They are each for the other quite equally. It is clear, however, that this prospective relation of essential oneness between the individual man and woman presupposes two things: — first, a basic marriage in the universal, a marriage of man as man with woman as woman; a marriage, in other words, of the essentially masculine with the essentially feminine. And second, this prospective relation of essential oneness between the individual man and woman presupposes a marriage in each individual, an at-one-ment with one's self that would make at-one-ment with another possible.[1]

Later in the address, Dickenson speaks to the union of the opposites and the need for women to be treated equally for the spiritual progress of humankind, stating

that it is equally beneficial to men that women be free
to pursue their own paths and learn personal responsibility. She emphasizes that for the sake of spiritual
growth and development, a woman must do things in
her own way, not in a man's way.

> Under a new impulse derived from woman herself,
> man is abdicating his external leadership, his exter-
> nal control over her. This he must do because his
> leadership and control in the past have expressed sep-
> aration and not union. He must do it for his own as
> well as her education into a higher idea of marriage.
> He must make the law in all its aspects toward her
> conform to this higher idea, to the truth that they are
> complementary to each other. Not "he for God only,
> she for God and him;" but both alike for God and
> each other. He must be willing to have her come
> down into the arena and share his contact with the
> world, since this is manifestly the providential school
> in which she is to learn her long neglected lesson of
> personal responsibility. She is to learn not only that
> she has feet of her own upon which she must stand;
> she must also learn for both their sakes how to stand
> upon them. The questions before us for solution
> today are pre-eminently social rather than political.
> They relate to the well-being of society, not merely
> to the success of party. They therefore include woman
> as she has never before been included, that is con-
> sciously, and in a way externally; in her way, how-
> ever, not in man's way. They are questions of the very
> life of man in the act of taking an upward step in his
> spiritual development.

Dickenson continued to develop her ideas when she returned home from the World's Parliament and often wrote on the subject of love and wisdom, supporting her position with passages from Swedenborg's work, such as *Divine Love and Wisdom* 14: "There can be no love except in wisdom, nor can there be any wisdom except from love." Of course, the view that masculine and feminine qualities are equally important was gaining acceptance throughout a wider public. Suffragist Elizabeth Cady Stanton expressed this thought in universal terms:

> The masculine and feminine elements, exactly equal and balancing each other, are as essential to the maintenance of the equilibrium of the universe as positive and negative electricity, the centripetal and centrifugal forces, the laws of attraction which bind together all we know of this planet whereon we dwell and of the system in which we revolve.[2]

Drawing upon other Swedenborgian concepts, Dickenson wrote for various periodicals. In the following piece, published in the *New Church Messenger* on April 8, 1896, she addresses the theme of what it means to be truly free:

> We are born free, that is, we are born with the two faculties of liberty and rationality, by means of which we may become free. We could not be born any other way, because God our Creator is freedom, and can give only of and from himself in creating. Thus, we find freedom everywhere impressed upon the universe. On her every plane, nature below man exhales freedom as the very breath of her life. All freedom is

of love we are told [Swedenborg, *Divine Providence* 73]. Nature loves the life divinely ordained for her. She freely and spontaneously lives it. That she can do no other than live it, in no wise alters the fact of freedom for her, in no wise disturbs her sense of delight. Freedom is the divine law of her life....

Is it with us as with nature? In common with nature, we are first born subject to the law of necessity. We, like her, have imperative needs, needs that like hers are answered for us. The child must receive all that he has from others, but he is happy in receiving and happy in his dependence. Subjection and dependence are the laws of his life, and, like nature, he has no sense of bondage in obeying it. He is free, and we have a sense of freedom in his presence as in that of nature. But this does not last for the child. By and by he grows away from the idea of subjection and dependence. Then he begins to learn the one lesson that he is created to learn, namely the meaning of the word "freedom." The one lesson, since the possibility of his learning all other needful lessons depends upon his learning this one. It is a long lesson and a hard one. Long and hard for him it has been for ages, is now, and will be until he is born of parents who have themselves learned the lesson. Then it will be easier.

Naturally, in the beginning of his self-conscious life, freedom means for him what it means for nature; what with certain comparatively unnoticed restrictions it has always meant for him, namely the liberty to do as he pleases. It means this because this is the divine meaning of the word. God does as He pleases. Nature does as she pleases. The child does as he pleases, and by and by the man learns that he, too, can do as he pleases and not come into bondage to himself and others, which is the first effect of his trying to do as he pleases. He learns the meaning for him of the word freedom. He learns that "all freedom is of love," for him, as for God, nature and the child, but that it is not as at first seems—freedom to love himself and seek himself, his selfish pleasure as an end, but freedom to love good and seek good in all his relations with himself and others. As he learns this lesson by the study and practice of divine truth, he also learns how "best to promote spiritual life in the Church." He finds for himself freedom to do as he pleases, in pleasing or loving to do the work to which he is providentially called—freedom, a God-given freedom in the midst of obstacles that oppose his work, and thus he becomes a power for freedom in the larger life of the organized church. Neither the individual nor the church can "work the works of God" in a state of bondage....

Genuine freedom, we must remember, does not consist in the liberty to love either good or evil, although we have this liberty (using it to love evil or self we come under the love of dominion which fetters our own activities, and as far as may be the activities of all with whom we are associated). Into this liberty, however, we must be born in order that through experience we may consent to be "born again" into the pure love of good, which, being one with the love of service, emancipates us from all desire to rule, and brings us more and more into the freedom, that is, into the love of God.

Women can best promote spiritual life in a church

by leading others into this freedom—the freedom of
the love of service. . . .

Lydia Fuller Dickenson is remembered for the love
and service she gave to her friends and community. Her
obituary, published in the August 1904 issue of the *New
Church Messenger* summarizes her forthright qualities:

> Mrs. Dickenson was a woman of rare intellectual
> powers. During her entire life she had been inter-
> ested in the people and movements that seemed to
> promise the coming of the dawn, of a new age for the
> world. She was temperamentally a believer in the
> new and the possibilities of coming good. Among
> other things, she was at one time greatly interested
> in the [women's] movement and in Fourierism, and
> never abated her keen sympathy with everything that
> related to the cause of women or the social perfec-
> tion of mankind.... She was always optimistic in her
> conviction concerning the possibilities of men and
> women, her influence was a brimming stream of sol-
> ace and encouragement. She made people believe in
> their better selves, and consequently her class work
> was never a mere social fad or pastime, but a real
> preaching of the gospel of practical helpfulness. More
> than a few women have testified to me of her
> abounding power to help....
>
> To those who knew Mrs. Dickenson best, her
> mental endowments did not seem paramount. Her
> woman's heart was her most honorable ornament.
> Her warm affections were rich and ample, and her
> living kindness made her a tower of strength to those
> who needed help. In very deed she was a mother in

Israel, and we cannot but rejoice at her summons to
a home-place in the Father's many-mansioned house.

NOTES

1 The entire text of Dickenson's speech, which is quoted
   in part in this chapter, can be found in L. P. Mercer, *The
   New Jerusalem in the World's Religious Congresses of 1893*
   (Chicago: Western New-Church Union, 1894), 82–90.

2 Elizabeth Cady Stanton, *The Original Feminist Attack of
   the Bible: The Woman's Bible* (New York: Arno Press,
   1974), 15.

Ednah Silver

CHAPTER SEVEN

MINISTRY OF GENTLENESS
Ednah Silver

*Faith in the life beyond has entered her understanding
of the world about her, showing everywhere the image
and promise of immortality. It has entered into her
interpretation of the experiences of life, its work, its
discipline, its blessings.*

From Memorial Service for Ednah Silver

EDNAH SILVER (1838–1928), educator and writer,
was born in Edwardsburg, Michigan, Her father,
the Rev. Abiel Silver, a Swedenborgian minister, served parishes in Contoocook, New Hampshire;
Wilmington, Delaware; Manhattan, New York; and Salem
and Roxbury, Massachusetts. Ednah participated in numerous theological discussions at an early age.

When the Silvers moved to New York in the 1860s,
Ednah began teaching Sunday School and describes her
experiences in her book *Sketches of the New Church in
America*:

I did not know a line of pedagogy, I had never been
near a normal school, I was without training in

forms, rules or systems, I was ignorant of child-psy-
chology as a science. But teachers are born and not
made. By instinct I kept completely within the children's range in the instruction given; they were eager
listeners, and volunteered questions worthy of a
forum: Would the little unbaptized boy next door
who had died go to heaven? Would the wicked father
ever see his child again?[1]

Silver's book offers personal glimpses of well-known
figures of nineteenth-century America, including
Howard Pyle, William Page, Mary Lathbury, Anna Cora
Mowatt, William Dean Howells, and Ralph Waldo
Emerson.

In 1893, Silver represented the Swedenborgian Church
at the World's Parliament of Religions in Chicago. The
New Jerusalem Church Congress, held in conjunction
with the World's Parliament, presented a forum where
Swedenborgian women could deliver papers on important topics of the day. After the morning sessions of the
religious congresses, the women participated in a series
of roundtable discussions that lasted all afternoon. Finding meaningful work, raising a family, and working for
personal, social, and political freedom were the main
topics. Addressing the realities of oppression and in-
equality, the speakers also brought out the underlying
themes of truth, freedom, liberty, justice, and peace in
different forms. In the paper she presented at the Religious Congress, Silver sheds light on the Swedenborgian
theme of usefulness and shares her views on the important aspect of "the ministry of gentleness," as she entitled her speech, that women can bring to the world:

If we go back 3,000 years we find one of the most remarkable characters in song or story — the classic deity, Minerva. Gradually evolved from the pagan mind in a period of unknown antiquity, she was vivified and strongly individualized by the genius of Homer, and became truly an immortal. The Greek philosophers looked upon her as symbolic; Homer's conception of her is more difficult to solve; but one thing is certain, within the panoply of the warrior maiden, beneath the supernatural authority of the goddess, one detects the woman.

While possessing regal power, scarcely second to that of Jupiter, and holding time and space under supernatural control, she is still seen at her best when presiding as a sort of pagan guardian angel over the young Telemachus. Other deities, even the wholly perverted Venus, can protect mortals from physical danger; Minerva saves from moral danger also. She coaxes, pets, chides, instructs, warns, encourages and inspires Telemachus in truly motherly fashion. She does not uniformly appeal to the higher motives as would a Christian guardian angel; nevertheless paganism was striving toward an ideal motherhood in Minerva's approximately enlightened ministry of gentleness.

A thousand years later the world saw this quality of gentleness exemplified in the life of Jesus Christ, a life whose luminous beauty stands in vivid relief against a background of violence and hate. With all power in heaven and on earth, He appeared neither in the wind nor in the earthquake, but under the gentle guise of infancy, leading men later by the ministry of lowly service, gentle teaching and kindly touch; laving the tired feet; pointing to the humility and ingenuousness typified by the child; laying his hands in blessing on the little ones.

Gentleness, although holding minor sway, still found expression. When the warrior, bruised and torn and helpless, was borne home, loved ones were there to undo some of the harm wrought. It was precisely the recognition of this softer element that constituted chivalry at its best; it was a tribute to gentleness and tenderness in an age of war and turbulence. It gave great impetus to — in fact I think it created — the worship of the Virgin Mary; especially as the Deity of medieval theology — a god of justice rather than of mercy — scarcely touched the finer sympathies....

At the same time woman's outward territory of usefulness is constantly enlarging. Once, she mitigated the horrors of war almost wholly in her own house, whether castle or hut, by nursing the wounded warrior. Now, a large field of organized work in this direction is open to her. Florence Nightingale entered it early, when moral courage and resolute will most supplemented sympathy and skill. Later came increased perfection of organization and wonderful executive ability under Clara Barton, also serving sufferers by earthquake, fire and flood.

But I wish to draw attention especially to work in which the motherly element in woman finds expression. The care of child-widows in India by Madame Ramabai, co-operation for the prevention of cruelty to children, all kindergartening, primary school instruction, Sunday-school instruction, Day Nurseries, assistance in Orphanages, aiding Working Girls' Clubs, the service of female physicians among homeless girls, Mothers' Meetings, where the educated woman works indirectly for children by instructing the un-tutored mother; the labor in the Woman's Christian Temperance Union to save young men from the per-ils of the saloon, the efforts through the White Cross Society to build higher the legal safeguards around young girls — all this is simply the function of moth-erhood enlarged; home, or the love of home, should be the inspiring center of it all.

The subject of the Woman's Movement, approached from the direction I have taken, seems to me to re-solve itself under two chief heads — Woman as a Mother, literal or representative, and Woman in her relation to Man. Regarding the former of these two vital relations, I would emphasize the point that the maternal attitude toward the young, the tempted or the friendless should in no degree supplant or weaken the direct home-life of the worker herself; the best vitality should of course be given to those nearest and dearest. No power of hers will ever be so potent as that exercised upon the plastic and sensitive na-ture of her own child, a nature of which she should possess the most sympathetic interpretation.

But the heart may be larger than the home. The key-note of all that is best in modern public effort is that love of God which finds new and more ex-tended expression in love toward humanity irrespec-tive of creed or race or nation. The ear of home must be more finely trained to detect the cry of need be-yond the threshold, the eye of home must be keener to see the way hither, the heart of home must be warmer to respond with sympathy, the mind of home must be better educated to decide wisely, the hand of home must be more skillful to fulfill the need. The

tendency in this direction on the part of both men
and women is simply that large and inclusive unsel-
fishness which we call public spirit, and of which the
Divine love is the inspiring force.[2]

Ednah Silver possessed the qualities of gentleness she
so often promoted, and continued to write, teach, and
serve her church and community until she died one
month after her ninetieth birthday. She spent her final
years in Roxbury, Massachusetts, and was an inspiration
to all who knew her. After her death, a 1928 article in
the *New Church Messenger* captured her spirit:

> Remembering Miss Silver as we have known her,
> slight in frame, and of late years almost frail, always
> cheerful, always alert and interested in fine things,
> knowing her own position and her own course and
> holding it with independence and courage, having
> her own hold upon the sources of power, there has
> been in our friend much to love, much to admire, and
> in her passing on there is a sense of work well done,
> and an assurance of readiness for the larger life of
> heaven....
>
> We will know her not as a memory only, but as a
> companion and fellow worker still, on the heavenly
> side, where sight is clearer, where bands are stronger,
> where hearts are braver, in the fuller consciousness of
> the Lord. Our look is not only backward, it is also
> forward. To the Divine love which has led her safely
> for ninety years, which has given her powers of use-
> fulness, and has filled her life with blessing, we intrust
> our friend in heaven.

NOTES

1 Ednah Silver, *Sketches of the New Church in America* (Boston: Massachusetts New Church Union, 1920), 195.

2 The entire text of Silvers's speech, which is quoted in part in this chapter, can be found in L. P. Mercer, *The New Jerusalem in the World's Religious Congresses of 1893* (Chicago: Western New-Church Union, 1894).

Mary Lathbury

CHAPTER EIGHT

MUSIC: LANGUAGE OF THE SOUL
Mary Lathbury

The harmonic of sounds and its varieties corresponds to states of joy and gladness in the Spiritual World, and the states of joy and gladness there come forth from the affections, which in that World are affections of good and truth.

Emanuel Swedenborg, *Arcana Coelestia* 8337

MARY ARTEMESIA LATHBURY (1841–1913), lyricist and poet laureate of Chatauqua, New York, was born in Manchester, New York. When she was almost twelve years old, Mary was told in a vision that she had a "gift of weaving fancies into verse, and a gift with the pencil of producing visions that come to your heart."[1] She remembered these prophetic words, and would fulfill her vision by writing from her inmost spirit for almost six decades.

When she was eighteen, Lathbury entered the School of Design in Worcester, Massachusetts. In the 1800s, society restricted women artists from developing professionally, and the schools catered to amateur artisans. After 1840, social changes took place that made a better education more accessible to women.

Success in any profession, however, required determination and dedication. Lathbury had the determination to complete her education and soon found respectable employment. She taught French and ornamental art at NewburyVermont Seminary; then in 1867, she joined the faculty of Drew Ladies' Seminary at Carmel, NewYork, where she further developed her literary and artistic skills.

By 1874, Lathbury served as assistant editor for several publications: *Sunday School Advocate*, *Classmate*, and *Picture Lesson Paper*. She also contributed to *St. Nicholas*, *Harper's Young People*, and *Wide Awake*. Her first book, *Fleda and the Voice*, was published in 1878, and her water colors were exhibited at the Academy of Design. Her second book, *Out of the Darkness into the Light,* illustrates and depicts the life of a young man as he overcomes temptation.

In the late 1800s, Lathbury became involved with the NewYork Chatauqua Institution, a popular adult-education movement that focused on arts and recreation. Devoted to the literary and scientific circles at the Chatauqua Institution, Mary blossomed as a musician and lyricist, with William F. Sherwin, Chautauqua's first music director, composing the melodies for many of her hymns. During the years of composing, she began to receive many requests for her poems and lyrics and became widely known as the poet laureate of Chautauqua. Her best hymns came from her Chatauqua experiences: "Arise and Shine," "Day is Dying in the West," and "Break Thou the Bread of Life," which is printed on the following page. This is still used as a communion hymn in many Swedenborgian church services.

Break Thou the bread of life, dear Lord to me,
As thou didst break the loaves beside the sea;
Within the sacred page I seek Thee Lord:
My spirit pants for Thee, O living Word.

Bless Thou the truth, O Lord, to me, to me,
As thou didst bless the bread by Galilee;
Then shall all bondage cease, all fetters fall;
And I shall find my peace, my All in All!

Thou' art the bread of life, O Lord, to me,
Thy holy word the truth that saveth me;
Give me to eat and live with Thee alone;
Teach me to love Thy truth, for Thou art love.

O send Thy Spirit, Lord, now unto me;
That He may touch my eyes, and make me see.
Show me the truth concealed within Thy Word,
And in Thy Book revealed I see the Lord.[1]

Lathbury's hymns often emphasized the themes of love
and unity and contributed to the developing ecumenical
movement of the 1800s. As she developed a broader view
of Christianity, other influences in her life contributed
to her poems and lyrics. Mary's brother, Clarence Lathbury, was a Swedenborgian minister; Mary also appreciated Swedenborg's works, using many of his concepts
in her hymns. She became a member of the Swedenborgian Church in Orange, New Jersey, in 1895 to explore
her beliefs further. Lathbury found that Swedenborg's
ideas were compatible with her own. Swedenborg described harmony as the blending of many feelings until

they appear as one, and felt that music puts feelings into harmonious order. When we are in touch with our feelings, we can experience our spiritual nature in the music we enjoy.[2]

Today, Lathbury's psalms, hymns, and spiritual songs bring harmony and order into the lives of those who experience her music. Her deep spiritual insight, her constant awareness of nature as a manifestation of its creator, her sense of spiritual truths in all that is written, and her appreciation of the close relationship between religion and science give her poems and lyrics a special depth of spirit that distinguishes them from others of the times.[3] In honoring this great poet and lyricist, the words of Everett Hale, author and nineteenth-century social reformer, best express her legacy:

> [Mary Artemesia Lathbury] has a marvelous lyric force, which not five people in a century show, and her chance of having a name two hundred years hence is better than that of most writers in America today.[4]

The hymns have outlived the woman who wrote them. Although her legacy is lost among most Swedenborgians, Mary Lathbury continues to be revered among Chautauquans. "Day is Dying in the West: Chautauqua" is still sung during Chautaugua's summer sessions. Bishop John Vincent, chancellor of Chautauqua University, stated in his 1913 tribute to Lathbury,

> She was both poetess and saint. Hers was a rare spirit. Some things she wrote will last for ages. . . . The old Chautauquans will never forget her and the new Chautauquans as they sing her songs will inbreathe

her devout, sweet spirit and thus be led into the deeper, richer life that Chautauqua seeks to represent and inspire.[5]

Notes

1 Mary Lathbury, *The Poems of Mary Artemesia Lathbury* (Minneapolis, Minnesota: Nunc Licet Press, 1915). The music for these lyrics can be found in *The Hosanna: A Song and Service Book for the Sunday School and Home*, 3rd revised edition (New York: Swedenborg Press, 1968), 101.

2 Wilson Van Dusen, "Music: Harmonic Elixir," *Chrysalis* IX, no. 2 (1994): 90–92.

3 Gladys E. Gray, "Mary Artemesia Lathbury: A 50th Anniversary Tribute," *The Hymn* 14, no. 2 (April 1963): 45.

4 Ibid, 37.

5 Lathbury, *Poems*, 12–13.

ARISE, ALL SOULS

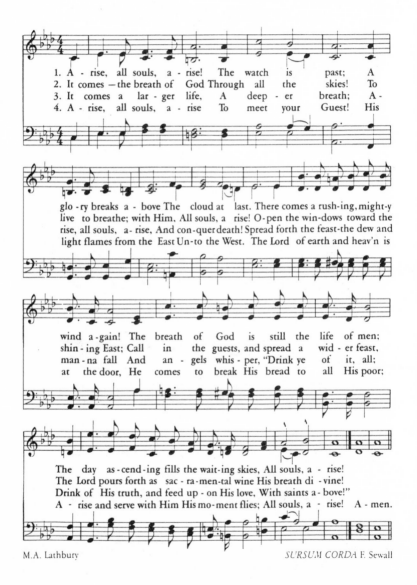

1. A - rise, all souls, a - rise! The watch is past; A
2. It comes — the breath of God Through all the skies! To
3. It comes a lar - ger life, A deep - er breath; A -
4. A - rise, all souls, a - rise To meet your Guest! His

glo -ry breaks a - bove The cloud at last. There comes a rush-ing, might-y
live to breathe; with Him, All souls, a rise! O-pen the win-dows toward the
rise, all souls, a- rise, And con-quer death! Spread forth the feast-the dew and
light flames from the East Un-to the West. The Lord of earth and heav'n is

wind a -gain! The breath of God is still the life of men;
shin - ing East; Call in the guests, and spread a wid - er feast,
man - na fall And an - gels whis - per, "Drink ye of it, all;
at the door, He comes to break His bread to all His poor;

The day as-cend-ing fills the wait-ing skies, All souls, a - rise!
The Lord pours forth as sac - ra-men-tal wine His breath di -vine!
Drink of His truth, and feed up - on His love, With saints a-bove!"
A - rise and serve with Him His mo-ment flies; All souls, a - rise! A - men.

M.A. Lathbury   *SURSUM CORDA* F. Sewall

Day is dying in the west

M. A. Lathbury   CHAUTAUQUA   W. F. Sherwin

1. Day is dy - ing in the west; Heaven is touch - ing
2. Lord of life, be - neath the dome Of the un - i -

earth with rest; Wait and wor - ship while the night
verse Thy home, Gath - er us, who seek Thy face,

Sets her eve - ning lamps a - light Through all the sky.
To the fold of Thy em - brace, For Thou art nigh.

REFRAIN

Ho - ly, ho - ly, ho - ly, Lord God of hosts! Heaven and earth are

full of Thee; Heaven and earth are prais - ing Thee, O Lord Most High!

3. While the deepening shadows fall,
Heart of Love, enfolding all,
Through the glory and the grace
Of the stars that veil Thy face,
Our hearts ascend.
Holy, holy, holy....

4. When forever from our sight
Pass the stars, the day, the night,
Lord of angels, on our eyes
Let eternal morning rise,
And shadows end!
Holy, holy, holy....

83

Selma Ware Paine

CHAPTER NINE

FOLLOWING ONE'S OWN PATH

Selma Ware Paine

*Whatever you love the most becomes your goal, and
you look to it in everything you do. This is present in
your motivation like the imperceptible current of a river
which carries you along even when you are thinking
of other things, for it is this which gives you life.*

Emanuel Swedenborg
New Jerusalem and Its Heavenly Doctrine 56

SELMA WARE PAINE (1847–1917), published writer
and musician, was born in Bangor, Maine,
where her father, an influential attorney, and her
mother, an artist and musician, encouraged her love of
art, literature, and music. Paine believed that each woman
needed to find her own way to be useful above and beyond the traditional role of wife or mother. Although
she never married or had children, she felt that moth-
erhood was an important role, but that it was, by its very
nature, a self-limiting career choice because when children get older, they no longer need full-time care. Paine
felt that the woman who raises her children without developing her own talents and skills can be left without

an outlet for her energies and talents. In addition, un-
married women, widows, and divorced women often
had to join the work force not just for self-fulfillment,
but out of necessity.

In developing arguments to support her views, Paine
stressed Swedenborg's concept of usefulness and his theory of the masculine and feminine nature. Each woman
or man should perform the role for which she or he is
best suited as an individual. If a woman believes she has
found her true path through life, she must follow it or
risk the consequences of going against her own nature.
Paine saw the need for changes in the views of how
women must live, and the works of Swedenborg gave
her a foundation for her journey to lead a useful life as
she followed her own true path.

Paine expressed her unique perspective on the concept of "uses" in her essay entitled "The Womanly Nature," which she presented at the Religious Congress at
the World's Parliament of Religions in 1893:

> As the lapidary, when he tests his jewels, puts aside
> those he knows are faultless, may we not, also, put
> aside from discussion, the admitted propositions:
> First, that, all other things being equal, the life of true
> marriage is higher and fuller than the single life, and,
> second, that the difference between men and women
> is innate, ineradicable and eternal? Then, as the jew-
> eler selects some brilliant gem that has a slight flaw,
> and says, "How beautiful it is, even if it is not perfect;"
> so I should like to have admitted that the single life
> lived aright offers more opportunities for usefulness
> and joy than any one being is able to improve. What
> is necessary is that there be the marriage of good and

truth within us. If it is there, we are quite independent of present external conditions. . . .

Often very fortunate is that woman whom her evident use leads in what her world recognizes in her day as the way of her womanly nature. It calls her, she must follow. She treads a beaten path. A strong arm provides for her the shelter she loves. It holds her back from the stifling dust, from the irksome toil of money-getting. Her troubles come. They are of a character men can understand. She struggles with them, and if she is victor, those about her rise and call her blessed.

But there are other women to whom their evident use says, "You cannot walk in the common highway. You are not most fit for that. You must pass, alone, through the forest. You must climb this mountain. You must descend into that dark and hidden valley." Or, perhaps it says, "Not for you the quiet of a sheltered home until you have earned it. For you, the glare of the counting-house; for you, to sweeten the fevered air of the hospital; for you, to fix visions of beauty on canvas; for you, to use the power of command in overseeing workmen; for you, to give in the pulpit the message that burns within you." Her duty calls her, she must follow. Perhaps the voice is stern and sounds like words of exile. Perhaps it is pleasing to her ear. That makes no difference. She is as worthy of honor as her sister if she obeys; as unworthy, if she refuses. Of one thing only let her beware, that she mistake not the voice. . . .

Is it not of the first importance that we recognize the temporal, the accidental, and accommodate ourselves to that under higher laws? The world moves always

in its changeless course around the sun, but on earth
the seasons come and go and no two are alike. In
some years our battle with the cold must be longer
than in others, and we must lay in more abundant
store. There is thus ever new variety under old perfect
laws. There is a constant creation of new needs. Old
forces must fill them, and we almost always find these
forces are waiting, throbbing with repressed activity.

That only can be the perfect Religion that holds
in it fidelity to the eternal and adaptability to the
new needs of life. How, tried by this standard, the
Divine Evangels shine out, how the Epistles take a
second rank. Nowhere in the Gospels is the place of
woman prescribed or limited. To her is each of its
everlasting teachings. She must not receive her seed
among thorns or in stony places....[1]

After her uplifting experience at the World's Parliament, Paine addressed many women's organizations, call-
ing the event "the most enlightening soul-event of the
century." Capturing the sentiments from her experience,
Paine tells her audiences about the Religious Congress:

Held in Chicago at the Memorial Art Palace on
Michigan Avenue with Great Lake Michigan at its
back, ...this building with its single gable and its long
wings, was to me very beautiful. Representatives of
any religion of the world could be heard for the des-
ignated three or four days. Each speaker was allowed
a half hour, one followed by another, and so it continued until, on the final evening, the crowd extended,
like a living thing of enormous length away down
Michigan Avenue. The attendance was impressive and

the enthusiasm for new ideas was contagious. A white-robed Buddhist Dharmapala came thirteen thousand miles to deliver his message. There was an overflowing feeling of brotherhood. Hospitality to everybody seemed to be the motto of the city. Hospitality to every thought was that of the Religious Congress. Many came over mountains and deserts, over sea and land to talk and listen, long-cherished hopes were made visible and audible realities. Clear, colorless, keen, the eyes deep-set and the expression attentive and kind, the form erect and spare....There they sat, the representatives of our theological and scholarly life. There were great moments, great hours in that hall, for which one should be grateful and better all his life.[2]

Lydia Augusta Carter, Paine's sister, described the essence of Selma's spiritual and intellectual life:

My sister Selma Ware Paine died in the winter of 1917, after a short illness. She had great strength of intellect and an unusually keen appreciation of all that was beautiful in the world of nature, art, music and literature. Hers was a gifted nature, one of rare beauty of character with the spiritual side predominant.

I have written much of father's interest in the New-Church teachings. With him these were a matter of intellect, a sure belief, and his whole life was guided by them. With her, these teachings became spiritualized and she breathed them in her poems and in her life. She never allowed her very frail body to limit her service for others. Her own happiness depended upon her ability to show some delicate attention to others, especially to those in sorrow and sickness, as well as to those in health and happiness.

Could I select one word that would represent the strongest element in her character it would be loyalty. She was loyal to things, loyal to friends, loyal to her home, loyal to her family and above all loyal to her church, but her keenness of appreciation for all that was beautiful must be emphasized.

When a mere child she began expressing herself in rhyme and was called upon to write verses for many a celebration, public and private, and never a family festival but brought with it offerings from her pen.

She passed nearly three years in Europe, studying music and the languages, afterwards adding to the latter during her life at home. She was one of the first to feel the power of Peer Gynt and to translate parts of it from the Danish. One of her latest treasures was a small, quaintly illustrated Bible written for our Penobscot Indians in their own language. Of this she made a very careful study.

Perhaps her greatest delight was in the study of Dante and this delight she shared with others, for she was an inspiring teacher to her friends, giving them many new thoughts by her interpretations of the Divine Comedy. "Terza Rima" shows her study of the construction of this work....[3]

After decades of using her innate gifts and talents to serve her community, Selma Ware Paine died in 1917, leaving behind a legacy of poetry, articles, translations, and essays to her descendants. A small volume of her poems, *Fugitive Verses*, was published in 1907 and is a treasured reminder of a woman who was able to follow her own path, in spite of the personal and social challenges of the times. In the last verse of her poem, "To the Wood Pewee," Paine sheds light on her thoughts regarding the continuity of life:

> Oh, gentle prophet of the year's decline,
> Why mark so soon the shortening of the days?
> The blooming Summer yet has maiden ways
> And, see, her cheek is roseleaf, fair and fine,
> Her breath is fragrant with the flowering vine,
> Her voice is full and firm with chorused lays.
> Why then your sweet untimely warning raise,
> Your autumn strain with summer song combine?
> And yet an added harmony you bring.
> There is a message in your music laid.
> Could summer song its full perfection reach
> Without a tone from Autumn and from Spring?
> Of present, past and future, life is made
> And what is perfect has a touch of each.

NOTES

1 The entire text of Paine's speech, which is quoted in part in this chapter, can be found in L. P. Mercer, *The New Jerusalem in the World's Religious Congresses of 1893* (Chicago: Western New-Church Union, 1894).

2 A. E. Scammon, et al, eds., *Round-Table Talks* (Chicago: Western New Church Union, 1985), 269–273.

3 Henry H. Carter, *The Discovery of a Grandmother* (Norwood, Mass.: Plimpton Press, 1920), 216.

Ellen Spencer Mussey

THE HEART OF SERVICE

Ellen Spencer Mussey

*True worship consists of fulfilling uses and, therefore,
expressing compassion in action....This means put-
ting our hearts into service to our country, our community, and our neighbor; it means acting with candor
toward our associates and performing our duties with
care according to our several abilities.*

Emanuel Swedenborg, *Arcana Coelestia* 7038

ELLEN SPENCER MUSSEY (1850–1936), attorney and
social reformer, was born in Geneva, Ohio.
When "Nellie" was twelve, her mother died, followed by her father and younger sister two years later.
After her father died, Nellie lived with various relatives
until 1869 when she moved to Washington, D.C., to live
with her brother Henry and sister-in-law Sarah Andrews
Spencer, a well-known suffragist. Ellen taught penmanship and various courses with her brother at the Spencer
Business College, named for her father, Platt, who had
developed the standard method of penmanship used in
the United States at the time. Ellen was only a teenager

93

when she became head of the woman's department at the college.

In 1869, Ellen Spencer met General Reuben Delavan Mussey, superintendent of the Sunday School at the Swedenborgian Church in Washington, and she became the Sunday School teacher of Mussey's two little girls. After General Mussey's wife died, Ellen and General Mussey began to spend time together, romance blossomed, and they were married in 1871. Within a short time, two boys were born to make a family of six.

The Musseys became a well-known Washington couple and attended many White House parties. They personally knew over a dozen presidents, among them Andrew Johnson, Ulysses Grant, Rutherford Hayes, James Garfield, Chester Arthur, and Grover Cleveland. Grace Hathaway, Mussey's biographer, describes President Grant's inaugural ball, one of the first social events that the Mussey's attended:

> The ballroom was gay with white muslin, evergreens, flags, and brilliant gas lights; and on the platform where President and Mrs. Grant were receiving were hundreds of canaries to greet the guests with song. But the room was glacial and the poor canaries, too frozen to sing, huddled pitifully in their cages, bills tucked under wings. Guests, blue and shivering, hurried through the formalities of the receiving line and back to dressing rooms to don furs and wraps. Men wore their overcoats, some of them even put on their hats, and the ladies swathed themselves in shawls.
>
> Announcement of supper, served before the dancing began, was received with a burst of enthusiasm because supper would be hot. The repast was a boun-

tiful one with plenty of champagne and claret punch, yet guests for the most part wanted neither of these. They ordered hot drinks, coffee, tea, and chocolate. Even these had to be taken quickly if taken hot for steaming foods were speedily cooled.

Because of the cold the Musseys did not stay for the dancing, and the party was a great disappointment to Mrs. Mussey.[1]

Ellen's disappointment did not last long because the Musseys also had a successful law practice and important business with prominent political figures. Unfortunately, law schools refused to admit Ellen because she was a woman, but she continued to study and work with her husband, taking on more and more responsibility as time passed. After General Mussey died in 1892, and after sixteen years of unofficially practicing law with her husband, Ellen Mussey had to stand on her own two feet as a lawyer. With years of experience and study behind her, she easily passed oral and written examinations and was admitted to the bar in Washington and officially became a lawyer in 1893.

Shortly after becoming an attorney, Ellen Mussey was appointed as a delegate to represent the Swedenborgian Church at the World's Parliament of Religions. An excerpt from her speech, illustrating Swedenborg's concept of uses, emphasizes the importance of women's active participation in social causes:

Dear sisters, let us fit ourselves and our daughters for a life of active use. Let us not be led astray by personal ambition, or love of ease. Let us remember that every soul is accountable to God, and that we must form our opinions, even though they differ from those we love best. Let us not be disputatious, but rather let us help our brothers to see that when they shut themselves away from the womanly influence, they are in fact closing the higher or celestial plane of their minds, and so preventing the doctrines of the Church from passing into life.[2]

Grace Hathaway described the air of social change that permeated the Chicago meetings and the importance Ellen attached to the World's Parliament:

The visit to Chicago was full of significance. The women's movement was gaining in momentum. The International Council of Women had recently been formed; also the National Council which had held its first triennial convention in 1891 with forty organizations of women represented; the General Federation of Women's Clubs was being organized; and for this World's Fair, Congress, through the skillful maneuvering of Susan B. Anthony and Elizabeth Cady Stanton, had actually authorized the appointment of a "Board of Lady Managers."

Headed by Mrs. Bertha Honore Palmer, this board planned a great World's Congress of representative women, which was held in connection with the Fair and which brought together the women of twenty-seven countries and 126 organizations. Thousands upon thousands of women, and men, too, attended the meetings. Women's activities and women's accomplishments were to the fore.

Even woman suffrage, so frowned upon that it had been given but one session, was arousing so much interest that extra meetings had to be held, and its valiant leader, Miss Anthony, once so ridiculed and defamed, became the veritable luminary of the Women's Congress. When she talked, crowds stormed the meetings, and when she appeared at other meetings, the crowd broke into the discourse of the speaker on the platform to do Miss Anthony honors.

Many women were being acclaimed. Never before had Mrs. Mussey seen such gatherings of gifted women and never had she heard of women receiving such plaudits. Her own former teacher and associate, Charlotte Emerson, now Mrs. Brown, was taking a prominent part in the General Federation of Women's Clubs. Mrs. Mussey felt inspired. And she saw clearly that organization was the secret of this advancement of women, that organization was the open sesame to power.

Up to this time she had not been a club woman, had had very little interest in societies other than those to which her husband had belonged, but she returned to Washington resolved to become active in women's organizations. She was fully aware of the importance of this professionally, for above all else, club work offered an opportunity to become known and if she was ever to be a success in the law, she must become known.

Fate Rides a Tortoise, 87–88

When Mussey returned home from the Parliament events, she continued her law practice and became more active in reform movements and in the causes for social change. Swedenborg's ideas gave depth to her own beliefs that women could be free to participate fully and

equally in society and lead useful lives. Wilson Van
Dusen's essay *Uses: A Way of Personal and Spiritual Growth*
best describes Swedenborg's concept of uses:

> The simplest and most powerful method for personal
> spiritual development in Swedenborg's theology lies
> in the idea of uses. Part of its beauty is its simplicity,
> which permits carrying it out in the midst of ordi-
> nary duties and labor, indeed, in any human act. It can
> be applied anywhere, anytime, by anyone. Part of its
> power lies in its wonderful concreteness. Much of
> religion has to do with masses of words and ideas.
> Use lies in concrete acts. Words are unnecessary. The
> very concrete immediacy of uses takes us out of our-
> selves, out into circumstances, out toward others and
> a larger world.[3]

Mussey continued to use her own gifts to help others.
In 1896 and 1897, she argued cases before the Supreme
Court and the United States Court of Claims and created new legislation regarding government appointees
and salaries. The American Red Cross was already an
important client, but with her impeccable reputation
and excellent work, Ellen's law practice began to blos-
som. Perhaps the most lasting result of these efforts was
the establishment of a law school with Emma Gillett,
which became the Washington College of Law in 1898.
Ellen Spencer Mussey became the first woman in the
world to become the dean of a law school and the first
six women law students were graduated in 1899.

Throughout the 1890s, Mussey campaigned to change
laws that discriminated against women. Now fully committed to women's causes, she wrote articles and letters

on reform subjects to various newspapers and periodicals. On June 1, 1898, Mussey's letter (with the headline "God Calls Each One") was published in the *New Church Messenger* :

> I am glad to see in the article signed by William H. Alden in the "Messenger" of May 18th a plea for leaving women in freedom to act according to the dictates of their own higher nature. It has always been a source of surprise to me that, especially in the churches, one sex should feel that they were justified in saying to the other, "Thus far shall you follow the dictates of your own conscience, and no further. Beyond that line, the Lord has given us sole control."
>
> It is fortunate for the great moral and social reform movements of the New Age that there have been men broad enough and women brave enough to cast aside this un-Christian-like attitude. What a loss it would have been to humanity if Florence Nightingale, Clara Barton, and Frances Willard had been afraid of overstepping the bounds of womanly decorum. In all the sixty-three nations who are parties to that great Red Cross treaty which owns a common brotherhood through all differences, the name of Clara Barton is known and loved, and yet if she had not been of strong purpose, she would have been turned aside from the mission by the mistaken view of what is really woman's sphere. Her mission is that of a woman whose family is the world, and she has performed its duties as only a woman could.
>
> Our brothers of the church do not desire to be unkind, or to overstep their own sphere, as they do when they dictate to women, but do they really see

the results of their own course of conduct? Not long
ago a lady member of the church was present at a
meeting of a neighboring Association. She was
deeply interested in the subject under discussion, and
the able papers being presented, and desired to present some thoughts when the question was open for
discussion. As a visitor, well-known to the presiding
officer as able to speak when called upon, he would
have undoubtedly extended the courtesy of an invi-
tation to join in the discussion, had she been a man.
Her heart burned within her, and after waiting pa-
tiently, she asked her hostess how it would affect others if she should join in the discussion, and the gentle
reply that she did not know how they would take it
caused her to keep silent. She went away from that
meeting feeling that she had been bound hand and
foot, that the spirit had moved her to speak, and that
her message had been suppressed.

Is it right to the Church and to the liberty of every
soul that this should be so? God made the bird to
sing. He has made women to think and feel, and
given them voices with which to be heard....

The work that God has given you to do is yours,
and the work that God has given me to do is mine.
Each soul is accountable to God alone, and let not
man step in between woman and the work to which
He may call her in his vineyard.

For the next three decades, Mussey continued to be
involved with women's issues, and continued to argue
divorce and custody cases. In 1933 she attended the
thirty-fifth commencement exercises of her law school,
where guest speaker Eleanor Roosevelt received from

Mussey an honorary degree of Doctor of Laws. Side by side, Mussey and Roosevelt led the procession together.

After this full life of service and accomplishment, Ellen Spencer Mussey, well into her eighties, died peacefully at her home on April 21, 1936.

NOTES

1 Grace Hathaway, *Fate Rides A Tortoise: A Biography of Ellen Spencer Mussey* (Chicago: The John C. Winston Company, 1937), 58. All further quotations from this work are cited in the text.

2 A.E. Scammon, et al, eds., *Round-Table Talks* (Chicago: Western New-Church Union, 1895), 190–191.

3 Wilson Van Dusen, "Uses: A Way of Personal and Spiritual Growth," in *The Country of Spirit: Selected Writings* (San Francisco: J. Appleseed & Co., 1992), 61.

APPENDIX

THE FOLLOWING WOMEN, according to autobiographies, biographies, or other sources, had an impact on the lives of women featured in *Lost Legacy*. Many were Swedenborgians or influenced by Swedenborg:

LOUISA MAY ALCOTT, 1832–1888
Best known for her classic *Little Women*, illustrated by Jesse Willcox Smith. A strong supporter of the anti-slavery movement. Also supported women's suffrage and temperance movements. Alcott's father, Bronson Alcott, was an avid reader of Swedenborg.

ELLEN ANDREWS, 1895–1953
Matron of Daniel Webster Home for Children. Member of the Boston Swedenborgian Church. Wrote for the *New Church Messenger*. Speaker at the Parliament of World's Religions.

ELIZABETH BLACKWELL, 1821–1910
Rejected by twenty-nine medical schools, she was finally accepted in 1847 at New York's Geneva College and became the first widely acknowledged female physician ·in the United States. Harriot Hunt, first woman to receive an honorary medical degree, was inspired by Blackwell's achievements.

ELIZABETH BARRETT BROWNING, 1806–1861
British poet. Best remembered for her collection of love poems, *Sonnets from the Portuguese*. Corresponding with many American women, she used her skills to promote the cause of freedom. Swedenborg's influence is directly seen in her lengthy work *Aurora Leigh*. Some of the women in *Lost Legacy* were inspired by her work and applauded *Aurora Leigh* in their autobiographies.

MARY CASSATT, 1844–1926
Impressionist painter, studied in France. Concentrated on mother-and-child theme. Her mural was displayed at the World's Columbian Exposition in 1893.

MARY SARGENT CONANT, 1850–1927
Married Dr. Thomas Conant. Granddaughter of Swedenborgian minister Samuel Worcester. Influential in the Gloucester Massachusetts New Church Society.

MARY BAKER EDDY, 1821–1910
Founded the Christian Science religion, based on the belief that illness is a mental condition rather than a physical one. Established the *Christian Science Monitor* in 1908. Sued for allegedly freely using material from Dr. Quimby's original work *Quimby Manuscript*, edited by Swedenborgian Horatio Dresser.

GEORGE ELIOT (MARY ANN EVANS), 1819–1880
British novelist who chose to write under a male pen name in the belief that her work would be taken more seriously. Best remembered for her novel *Middlemarch*. Inspiration for American women.

ANNIE ADAMS FIELDS, 1834-1915
Author and literary figure. Social welfare worker born in Boston, Massachusetts. Married to editor of the *Atlantic*, James T. Fields. Close friendship with writer Sarah Orne Jewett.

(SARAH) MARGARET FULLER, 1810–1850
Editor for transcendentalist periodical *The Dial*. Literary critic, writer, and foreign correspondent. Influenced by Swedenborg's writing and credited him in her book *Woman in the Nineteenth Century*, for being one of the influences for her in her plight for women's equality. Drowned in a shipwreck on a voyage back to America from Italy.

CHARLOTTE PERKINS GILMAN, 1860–1935
Wrote *Women and Economics* in 1898. Family belonged to a Swedenborgian Church in Boston, Massachusetts. Known for classic novel *The Yellow Wallpaper*.

SARAH GRIMKE, 1792–1872
An early abolitionist and gifted orator who also fought for the right of women to give public speeches. Dr. Harriot Hunt dedicated her autobiography *Glances and Glimpses* to her.

JULIA WARD HOWE, 1819–1910
Reformer, suffragette, abolitionist, and American writer. Wrote lyrics to the *Battle Hymn of the Republic*. Spent long quiet mornings sailing from Italy to the United States reading Swedenborg's *Divine Love and Wisdom*. Howe's new attitude toward Christianity was derived

from Swedenborg's theory of the divine human. Howe wrote a biography on Margaret Fuller.

ALICE JAMES, 1848–1892
Nineteenth-century writer, best-known for her work *The Diary of Alice James.* Belonged to a woman's club with other Swedenborgian women. Daughter of Swedenborgian Henry James Sr.; sister of Henry James Jr., writer; and William James, philosopher and writer.

HELEN KELLER, 1880–1968
Blind and deaf, Keller learned to read Braille, speak, and use a typewriter after years of study with her teacher Anne Sullivan Macy. Graduated from Radcliffe College in 1904 and became politically active. Author of book titled *My Religion*, which shows the impact Swedenborg's writing had on her life.

LUCRETIA COFFIN MOTT, 1793–1880
Helped establish the American Anti-Slavery Society in 1833, but was barred from the international anti-slavery convention in London in 1840 because she was a woman. Focused on the woman's suffrage movement. In 1848, Elizabeth Cady Stanton and Mott organized the Women's Rights Convention at Senaca Falls, New York. Worked closely with Harriot Hunt.

MARY SARGEANT NEAL GOVE NICHOLS, 1810–1884
Writer, editor, married by a Swedenborgian clergyman and had close ties with the Swedenborgian community. Claimed to have gift of healing. Became involved with mysticism and "water cure."

ELIZABETH EMILY PARSONS, 1824–1880
Born in Taunton, Massachusetts. Eldest daughter of
Theophilus Parsons and Catherine Amory Chandler
Parsons. Active in the Swedenborgian Church. Top su-
pervisor of Civil War nurses.

ELIZABETH PALMER PEABODY 1804–1894
Education reformer born in Billerica, Massachusetts.
Member of transcendentalist group with Margaret Fuller,
Ralph Waldo Emerson, Bronson Alcott, and others.

LYDIA SCOTT ROTCH, 1782–1863
Philanthropist and member of the Bridgewater Swedenborgian Society (1831–1846) and Boston Society (1846–
1863). Endowment of Rotch Fund continues to support many educational projects, including the publication of *Lost Legacy*.

ELIZABETH CADY STANTON, 1815–1902
Organized the 1848 women's rights convention at
Seneca Falls with Lucretia Mott; physician Harriot Hunt
worked with her and spoke at various events. Co-founded
the National Woman Suffrage Association with Susan
B. Anthony. Wrote *The Woman's Bible* in 1895.

MARY WALSH, 1810–1882
Married to Henry James Sr.; mother of William James,
Henry James Jr., and Alice James. Family was influenced
by Swedenborg's works.

BIBLIOGRAPHY

Bacon, Margaret Hope. *Mothers of Feminism: The Story of Quaker Women in America*. San Francisco: Harper & Row, 1986.

Beede, Vincent Van Marier. "Mary A. Lathbury, Her Life and Lyrics." *The Chatauquan*, xxx, October 1899: 34-40.

Bell, Michael Davitt. *Jewett*. New York: The Library of America, 1994.

Blanchard, Paula. *Sarah Orne Jewett: Her World and Her Work*. Reading, Mass.: Addison-Wesley Publishing Company, 1994.

Block, Maguerite. *The New Church in the New World*. New York: Swedenborg Publishing Association, 1984.

Brock, Erland, et.al. *Swedenborg and His Influence*. Bryn Athyn, Penna.: The Academy of the New Church, 1988.

Brooks, Angeline. "The Work of Mary A. Lathbury." *Sunday Republican* (Springfield, Mass.), October 2, 1910.

Browning, Elizabeth Barrett. *Letters to Her Sister, 1846-1859*. London: J. Murray, 1929.

Bukovinsky, Janet. *Women of Words: A Personal Introduction to Thirty-Five Important Writers.* Philadelphia: Running Press, 1994.

Carter, Henry H. *The Discovery of a Grandmother.* Norwood, Mass.: Plimpton Press, 1920.

Child, Lydia Maria (Francis). *An Appeal in Favor of That Class of Americans Called Africans.* Boston: Allen and Ticknor, 1834.

———. *The Frugal Housewife.* Boston: Marsh and Capen, and Carter and Hendee, 1829.

———. *Hobomok, A Tale of Early Times.* Boston: Cummings, Hilliard, 1824.

———. *The Letters of Lydia Maria Child.* Boston: Houghton Mifflin and Company, 1883. Reprinted Boston: AMS Press, Inc., 1969.

———. *Letters from New York: Second Series.* New York: Francis and Co., 1847.

———. *The Progress of Religious Ideas, Through the Successive Ages.* 3 vols. New York: C. S. Francis, 1855.

———. *Selected Letters, 1817-1880.* Edited by Milton Meltzer. Amherst, Mass: The University of Massachusetts Press, 1982.

Dole, George F. *A Thoughtful Soul: Reflections From Swedenborg.* West Chester, Penna: Swedenborg Foundation, 1995.

Donavan, Josephine. *Sarah Orne Jewett.* New York: Frederick Ungar Publishing Co., 1980.

Dubuy, Georges, and Michelle Perot, eds. *A History of Women: Emerging Feminism from Revolution to World War*. Cambridge, Mass.: Belknap Press, 1993.

Edmonson, Catherine, ed. *365 Women Who Made a Difference*. Holbrook, Mass: Adams Media Corporation, 1997.

Fuller, Margaret. *The Portable Margaret Fuller*. Edited by Mary Kelley. New York: Penguin Books, 1994.

Gilbert, Sandra M., and Susan Gubar, eds. *The Norton Anthology of Literature by Women*. New York: W. W. Norton & Company, 1985.

Gilman, Charlotte Perkins. *The Yellow Wallpaper*. Rpt. New York: The Feminist Press, 1966

Hathaway, Grace. *Fate Rides a Tortoise: A Biography of Ellen Spencer Mussey*. Chicago: The John C. Winston Company, 1937.

Howe, Julia Ward. *Margaret Fuller*. Westport, Conn.: Greenwood Press Publishers, 1883. Reprinted 1970.

Hunt, Harriot K., M. D. *Glances and Glimpses; or Fifty Years Social, including Twenty Years Professional Life*. Boston: Jewett and Company, 1856.

Hymowitz, Carol, and Michaele Weissman. *A History of Women in America*. New York: Bantam, 1978.

James, Edward T., et. al., ed. *Notable American Women: A Biographical Dictionary*. Cambridge, Mass.: Harvard University Press, 1971.

Jewett, Sarah Orne. *Letters of Sarah Orne Jewett*. Edited by Annie Fields. Boston: Houghton, Mifflin, 1911.

_____. *Novels and Stories: Deephaven, A Country Doctor, The Country of the Pointed Firs, Dunnet Landing Stories, Selected Stories and Sketches*. New York: The Library of America, 1994.

Julian, John, ed. *Dictionary of Hymnology*. Two volumes. Grand Rapids, Michigan: Kregel Publications, 1985.

Karcher, Carolyn L. *The First Woman in the Republic: A Cultural Biography of Lydia Maria Child*. Durham, North Carolina: Duke University Press, 1994.

Keller, Helen. *My Religion*. New York: Doubleday, Doran & Company, 1928.

_____. *Light in My Darkness*. Edited by Ray Silverman. West Chester, Penna.: Swedenborg Foundation, 1994.

Larsen, Robin, et al, eds. *Emanuel Swedenborg: A Continuing Vision*. New York: Swedenborg Foundation, 1988.

Lathbury, Mary A. *The Poems of Mary Artemesia Lathbury*. Minneapolis, Minn.: Nunc Licet Press, 1915.

Lerna, Gerda. *The Creation of Feminist Consciousness: From the Middle Ages to Eighteen–Seventy*. New York: Oxford University Press, 1993.

Lunardini, Christine. *What Every American Should Know About Women's History*. Holbrook, Mass.: Adams Media Corporation, 1997.

Mercer, L. P. *The New Jerusalem in The World's Religious Congresses of 1893*. Chicago: Western New-Church Union, 1894.

Mowatt, Anna Cora. *Autobiography of An Actress or, Eight Years on the Stage.* Boston: Ticknor, Reed, and Fields, 1853.

_____. *Fashion, Or Life in New York. Feedback, (1845).* New York: Theatrebooks and Prosper Press, 1996.

_____. *The Lady of Fashion.* Edited by Eric Wollencott Barnes. New York: Charles Scribner's Sons, 1954.

_____. *Plays.* Boston: Ticknor and Fields, 1854.

Nudelman, Edward. *Jessie Willcox Smith: American Illustrator.* Gretna, La.: Pelican Publishing Company, 1990.

Pitz, Henry C. *Howard Pyle: Writer, Illustrator, Founder of the Brandywine School.* New York: Bramhall House, 1965.

Scammon, A. E., et al, eds. *Round-Table Talks.* Chicago: Western New Church Union, 1895.

Schnessel, S. Michael. *Jessie Willcox Smith.* New York: Crowell, 1977.

Silver, Ednah. *Sketches of the New Church in America.* Boston: Massachusetts New Church Union, 1920

Silverthorne, Elizabeth. *Sarah Orne Jewett: A Writer's Life.* Woodstock, New York: The Overlook Press, 1993

Smith, Jessie Willcox. *The Jessie Willcox Smith Mother Goose.* New York: Derrydale Books, 1986.

Stanley, Michael, editor. *Emanuel Swedenborg: Essential Readings.* Wellingborough, England: Crucible, 1988.

Stanton, Elizabeth Cady. *The Original Feminist Attack of the Bible: The Woman's Bible.* 1895; rpt. New York: Arno Press, 1974.

Warmer, Carolyn. *Treasury of Women's Quotations.* New York: Prentice Hall, 1992.

Willard, Frances E. *Glimpses of Fifty Years, 1839-1889.* Philadelphia: H. J. Smith Co., 1889.

Woofenden, Louise. "Famous Readers of Swedenborg: Anna Ogden Mowatt." *Five Smooth Stones,* September 1985.